Costa del Sol
& Andalucía

Berlitz Publishing Company, Inc.
Princeton   Mexico City   London   Eschborn   Singapore

Berlitz Trademark Reg. U.S. Patent Office and other countries
Marca Registrada

Text:	Norman Renouf
Editor:	Erica Spaberg Keirstead
Photography:	Chris Coe except pages 3, 5, 45, 47, 49, 54, 85, 91, 92 by Neil Wilson
Cover Photo:	Chris Coe
Photo Editor:	Naomi Zinn
Layout:	Media Content Marketing, Inc.
Cartography:	Raffaele De Gennaro

ISBN 2-8315-7692-X

Printed in Italy

030/107 RP

CONTENTS

• A (☞ in the text denotes a highly recommended sight

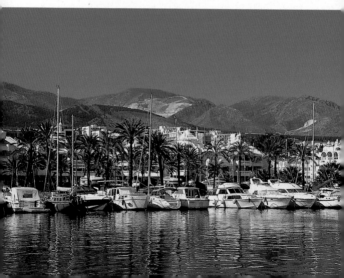

Costa del Sol & Andalucía

THE REGION AND
ITS PEOPLE

For thousands of years, the people of the Costa del Sol, except when invaded or in times of war, went about their business oblivious of the concerns of the outside world. In the last half of the 20th century that changed dramatically, however, when the Costa transformed itself from a collection of sleepy towns and fishing villages into the playground of the world.

Strung along the southern coast of Spain between Gibraltar in the southwest and Almería to the east, this Mediterranean coastline encompasses parts of four (Cádiz, Málaga, Granada, and Almería) of the eight provinces of Andalucía, Spain's southernmost autonomous community. The other provinces are Huelva, adjoining Portugal and the Atlantic Ocean, and the landlocked Sevilla, Córdoba, and Jaén. Surprisingly, the beaches on the Costa del Sol are not wide, with miles of yellow sand, as on the Atlantic Ocean. Rather, never far from the mountains and in some sections directly next to them, they are usually comprised of a dull gray sand that has been formed by the erosion of these same mountains. In fact, many of the beaches aren't particularly attractive, often running parallel to the busy N-340 highway that runs the length of the Costa del Sol. In summer, some of them can be more than a little crowded.

What, then, attracts millions of visitors from every corner of the globe? Well, for a start, bountiful sunshine almost year-round. The Costa del Sol has an average of 320 cloud-free days a year. And because the region is protected by an almost endless wall of mountains—the Sierra Nevada to the east of Málaga and the Serranía de Ronda to the west—it is spared the harsh, arid heat of the inland plateau. Temperatures in the summer rarely rise above 30ºC (86ºF). Second, such a climate encourages an easygoing atmosphere; the locals, despite having had their way of life changed dramatically, still retain a gregarious, garrulous, and generous nature for the most part. Like all Spanish, the Andalucíans are a tolerant people. Outnumbered by foreigners on their home territory, they take the tourist invasion in their stride, welcoming the influx of cash and the enhanced opportunities that it brings.

Málaga's international airport is the primary gateway to the Costa del Sol that, for purposes of explanation, can be subdivided into two sections: west and east of Málaga. The more familiar image of the Costa del Sol is to be found west of Málaga, where development reaches far back from the beaches. In the original tourist boom town of Torremolinos, high-rise hotels and squat apartment blocks loom above the waterfront promenade, and the bustling back streets are lined with pubs, clubs, discos, chip shops, curry houses, and other things British. The apartment complexes around the marina at Benalmádena, however, are far more attractive than the unregulated sprawl found in its near neighbor, and show what can be achieved with a little foresight. Fuengirola is similar to, but rather more staid than, Torremolinos.

Marbella, though, is very different. The original playground of the sixties' jet set and the upmarket showcase of the Costa del Sol, Marbella was first put on the map by Prince Alfonso von Hohenlohe in the 1950s. Today, movie stars, oil-rich Arab potentates, and other celebrities keep it in the news. In more recent years, though, neighboring Puerto Banús has emerged as the place to be seen. Huge magnificent yachts may be admired in the marina, gourmet restaurants line the harbor, and sophisticated stores abound. Toward Estepona, hotels and apartment complexes diminish

The architecture throughout the Costa del Sol reflects the 800 years that the area was ruled by the Moors.

in number, but are no less stylish, as stretches of empty beach and green hillsides claim the landscape.

Continuing on, the familiar silhouette of the Rock of Gibraltar dominates the skyline. Should you want to investigate further, it is accessible by the road that leads off the N-340 at San Roque and ends at La Linea de la Concepción, the border with Gibraltar. Across the bay, Algeciras is the gateway to North Africa, which can be seen, albeit often through a haze, just across the Strait of Gibraltar. Still better views are to be had from the *mirador* (viewpoint) on the hills as the road winds around to Tarifa, the end of the Costa del Sol.

The eastern part of the Costa, from Málaga to Almería, is quieter and less intensively developed. Rincón de la Victoria and Torrox are the first couple of resorts, but you will have to travel to Nerja, the largest resort on this stretch of coast, to find anything approaching those in the western section. Yet, even here, the ambience is considerably quieter. Very soon, after the mountains begin to drop precipitously into the sea, wonderful views abound from the road, with family resorts like La Herradura and Almuñécar nestled in bays.

This stretch of the Costa del Sol, in the Provincia de Granada, is now known as the Costa Tropical. Motril sits in the middle of an unexpectedly lush green delta planted variously with avocados, citrus fruits, sugar cane, bananas, and bamboo, and

is guarded to the west by Salobreña and its Moorish castle. Motril to Adra is a conservation area and, besides being far and away the least built up of any area on the whole Costa del Sol, it is also, scenically, the most dramatic. Conversely, the route across the plain after leaving Adra is the dreariest along the Costa del Sol. Fortunately, the mountains again meet the sea near the town of Aguadulce, enlivening the last few kilometers into the city of Almería.

Visitors can explore many charming sights, such as the Plaza de España, in Sevilla.

There was some negative publicity in the 1980s, stemming from concerns about uncontrolled development, traffic congestion, dirty beaches, polluted seas, and a rising crime rate. These concerns have been addressed and recent years have brought a vigorous and effective campaign to clean up the beaches and water, to build better roads and bypasses, and to curtail crime.

The attributes that led to the initial development of the Costa del Sol remain as major attractions. Travel to the Costa is inexpensive and easy, it has good beaches, and the sun can be relied upon to shine nine days out of ten. The Costa del Sol also boasts an extensive array of attractions that are difficult to find in such close proximity elsewhere, and is one of the liveliest and most cosmopolitan resort areas in the world. What other place can boast of visitors ranging from the King of Saudi Arabia to English lager louts, and all others in between?

Those visitors who are willing to investigate beyond the beaches will find a collection of charming whitewashed villages. Beyond the mountains are numerous ancient towns whose histories are known throughout the world. There's Sevilla, famed for its bullfights and flamenco dancers; Córdoba, the first capital of Moorish Spain; and Granada, capital of the last Moorish kingdom in Spain and home of the magnificent Alhambra palace. But this is also where you'll find Jerez de la Frontera, headquarters of the world's sherry trade; Ronda, with its stunning gorge and 18th-century bullring; and Cádiz, founded by the Phoenicians and considered the oldest city in Spain.

It is these Andalucían cities that offer those quintessential images that come to mind when Spain is mentioned—places that are steeped in history, with bullfights, flamenco dancers, and sun-drenched landscape.

A BRIEF HISTORY

T he southern part of Spain is at a geographical crossroads: It is the gateway between the Mediterranean and the Atlantic, and the crossing point between Africa and Europe. The strategic importance of its location has given rise to a long and turbulent history.

The earliest evidence of human occupation is provided by the Paleolithic cave paintings, some 25,000 years old, in the Cueva de la Pileta. Neolithic peoples arrived on the scene in the fourth millennium B.C., leaving behind signs of early attempts at agriculture and fragments of their pottery. Tribes of Iberians from North Africa crossed over into Spain around 3000 B.C., and initiated Spain's first experiments in architecture; Spain's oldest structure stands near Antequera, a dolmen burial chamber known as the Cueva de Romeral. After 900 B.C., wandering bands of Celts entered the peninsula from northern Europe, and brought to the area their knowledge of bronze and iron work. As they moved farther south, the Celts merged with the Iberians, and began to build walled villages along the coast.

Traders and Colonizers

About the same time this was taking place, the Phoenicians were already venturing across the Mediterranean from their homeland in present-day Lebanon. They reached Spain by about 1100 B.C., founding many trading settlements in the land they called *Span* or *Spania*. The first was Gades (modern Cádiz), followed by Malaka (now Málaga), and Abdera (Adra) on the Costa del Sol. Contact with the sophisticated Phoenicians introduced the Celt-Iberians to the concept of currency.

After about 650 B.C., Greek traders entered the competition to exploit Spain's rich mineral deposits and fertile land. Their influence was short-lived, although the olive and the grape, both Greek legacies, soon became important, well-tended crops.

The Carthaginians, a North African people related to the Phoenicians, subsequently took over much of southern Spain, beginning with Cádiz in precisely 501 B.C. They extended their influence along the River Guadalquivir to Sevilla, then to Córdoba. On the coast, they founded the city of Carteya, overlooking the Bay of Algeciras (240 B.C.). Carthage, challenged by Rome in the First Punic War (264–241 B.C.), lost most of its Spanish possessions to Iberian attacks. But its fortunes changed with an initial victory in the Second Punic War (218–201 B.C.).

Southern Spain flourished and was peaceful under the rule of the scholarly Moors.

Emboldened, the Carthaginian general Hannibal decided to advance on Rome. He led one of history's great military marches from Spain into Italy, crossing the Pyrenees and the Alps on the way. The Romans invaded Spain to cut off Hannibal's supply route — and stayed there for some 600 years.

Roman Rule

It took the Romans two centuries to subdue the Iberians, but in the end most of the peninsula was incorporated into their new colony of Hispania. The south formed part of the province of Baetica, virtually identical to today's Andalucía, with Córdoba its capital.

The Roman presence had a far-reaching influence on the country. A road network was constructed (the Via Augusta ran the length of the south coast on its way to Rome) and bridges, aqueducts, villas, and public buildings were added to the list of their achievements. The introduction of the Latin language (from which modern Spanish developed), Roman law (the basis of Spain's legal system), and, eventually, Christianity brought about stability and a degree of unity.

Eventually the Roman Empire began to crumble. The Romans withdrew from Spain. This left the country to be overrun by various barbarian tribes, especially the Vandals. The Visigoths who, for some 300 years, controlled much of

The walls of Málaga's Alcazaba surround a partially restored palace and offer a panoramic view of the nearby sea.

southern Spain, eventually dominated these tribes. Ultimately, the Visigothic kingdom proved unstable. The monarchy was elective, rather than hereditary, which led to disputes over succession to the crown; and in one of these, the disaffected party looked to North Africa for an ally.

Moors and Christians

In A.D. 711, some 12,000 Berber troops landed at Gibraltar, beginning a period of Moorish rule that was not broken by the Christians until nearly 800 years later. Following their victory at the Battle of Guadalete, the Moors (the name given to the Muslims in Spain) carried all before them. They pushed the Visigoths into the northern mountains, and within ten years most of the country had fallen to Islam. To this day, Almuñécar, Tarifa, Algeciras, Benalmádena, and several other southern towns are known by their Arabic names. So is Andalucía, for that matter, originally the Moorish kingdom of Al Andalus.

The Moors chose Córdoba as their seat of government, and from the 8th to the very early 11th centuries, it ranked as one of the great cities of the world. The city was capital of the independent caliphate of Córdoba, founded by Abd-er-Rahman III in 929. Under the caliphs, southern Spain knew prosperity and peace, for the Moors were relatively tolerant rulers and taxed non-believers rather than trying to convert them. Intellectual life flourished, and great advances were made in science and medicine.

With the introduction of a sophisticated irrigation system, crops such as rice, cotton, and sugar cane were cultivated for the first time on Spanish soil, as well as oranges, peaches, and pomegranates. The manufacture of paper and glass was another Moorish innovation. Skilled engineers and architects, the Moors built numerous palaces and fortifications.

As superb craftsmen they excelled in the production of ceramics and tooled leather, as well as delicate silverware.

The ensuing fall of Córdoba was as remarkable as its rise. In 1009, the caliphate splintered into a number of small kingdoms called *taifas*, which were constantly at war. The Christians in the north, seeing the enemy weakened and divided, captured the *taifa* of Toledo. Under threat of attack, the other taifas sought help from the Almoravids, fanatical Berber warriors. The Berbers marched against the Christians in 1086, and went on to reduce Moorish Spain to a province of their own North African Empire.

For a time, therefore, the affairs of Muslim Spain were administered from the Almoravid headquarters in Granada, until they lost their grip on the peninsula, softened by their life of ease in Andalucía. The pattern repeated itself a century later when the Moors invoked the aid of the Almohads in 1151. These primitive tribesmen, who came from the Atlas Mountains of Morocco, soon made themselves the masters of southern Spain. They constructed major fortifications, such as Sevilla's Alcázar, endowing the Moors with sufficient strength to resist the Christian forces a while longer.

The fortunes of the Moors and Christians swayed back and forth until 1212, when the Christians gained their first decisive victory at Las Navas de Tolosa in northern Andalucía. The Christians gradually captured and annexed the former bastions of Moorish rule; in 1236, Córdoba fell to James the Conqueror, followed by Sevilla in 1248. The Moors were in retreat, retrenching along the coast and withdrawing to the security of their strongholds in Ronda and Granada.

In military disarray and political decline, Moorish Spain nevertheless saw another two centuries of brilliance under the Nasrid dynasty, founded in Granada by Mohammed I in 1232. Refugees from Córdoba and Sevilla flooded into the city, bringing with them their many talents and skills and adding to the city's brilliance. The magnificent palace of the Alhambra provided the setting for a luxurious court life dedicated to the pursuit of literature, music, and the arts.

Yet, the Moorish fortresses along the coast soon came under attack. Sancho IV took Gibraltar in 1310, but the Christians later relinquished their prize, and the Moors held on to it until 1462. In the 1480s, the Christians launched a new offensive; Ronda capitulated to the sovereigns Ferdinand and Isabella in 1485, followed by Málaga in 1487 and Almería in 1488. And all Christendom gave thanks when Granada was finally conquered in 1492.

The Golden Age

With the triumph of Christianity, the country was united under the Catholic Monarchs (*Los Reyes Católicos*), a title conferred by Pope Alexander VI on Ferdinand II of Aragón and Isabella I of Castile. Also in 1492, Cristobal Colón (Christopher Columbus) discovered the New World in the name of the Spanish crown. Fanatical in their religious zeal, the king and queen expelled all Jews who refused to convert to Christianity in the same year, and the Moors followed in 1502. The rulers thus reneged on the promise of religious freedom they had given when Granada surrendered. With the Jews who left Spain went many of the country's bankers and merchants, and with the Moors, a good number of its agriculturists and laborers. The converted Jews (*conversos*) and Moors (*Moriscos*) who remained in Spain were viewed with suspicion by the Inquisition, which had been established by the Catholic Monarchs to stamp out heresy. Many were condemned to death, and still more fled the country to escape persecution.

The 16th century was glorious for Spain, with the conquest of the New World bringing much prestige and wealth. In 1503, the Casa de Contratación in Sevilla was awarded a monopoly on trade with Spain's territories in the Americas. For more than two centuries, Sevilla was the richest city in Spain.

By comparison, the coastal settlements languished, and were subject to frequent raids by Barbary pirates. Under constant threat for more than 200 years, the population drifted inland, taking refuge in fortified towns and villages hidden in the foothills of the Sierras.

As Emperor, Charles V of the Holy Roman Empire, the first Habsburg Spanish king, turned his attention to events in Europe. Between 1521 and 1556, he went to war with France four times, squandering the riches of the Americas on endless military campaigns. Charles also had a weakness for such costly projects as his vast Renaissance palace on the grounds of the Alhambra, which he commissioned in 1526. Taxes imposed on the Moors served to finance the building works, which eventually had to be abandoned for lack of funds when the Moriscos revolted 12 years into the reign of Philip II (1556–1598). The king dispatched his half-brother, Don Juan of Austria, to quell the rebellion, which ended in 1570 with the defeat of the Moriscos and their eventual dispersal. In 1588, Philip II prepared to invade England, only to be repulsed when the English navy destroyed Spain's previously invincible Armada.

The defeat marked the start of a long decline. Philip's military forays and his expensive taste left Spain encumbered with debts. Participation in the Thirty Years' War under Philip III led to further financial difficulties and to another debacle in 1643, when Spanish troops were defeated by the French at Rocroi in Flanders, never to regain their prestige.

French Ascendancy

Spain's internal affairs became the concern of the other great powers after Charles II died without an heir. The Habsburg

Archduke Charles of Austria challenged France's Philip of Bourbon in the ensuing War of the Spanish Succession. Gibraltar was the scene of some fierce fighting in 1704, when Great Britain captured the Rock on behalf of Austria. Under the terms of the Treaty of Utrecht, which also confirmed Philip's right to the Spanish throne, Spain was finally forced to relinquish its claims to Gibraltar in 1713.

Nearly a hundred years later, during the Napoleonic Wars, Spanish ships fought alongside the French fleet against Lord Nelson at Cape Trafalgar (see page 46). But as the wars continued, Napoleon, distrustful of his ally, forced the Spanish king Ferdinand VII to abdicate in 1808, and imposed his brother, Joseph, as king. He then sent thousands of troops across the Pyrenees to subjugate the Spanish, who promptly revolted.

The Rock of Gibraltar lies at the westernmost point of the Mediterranean — once thought to be the edge of the world.

The gardens at the Alcázar in Sevilla are a perfect complement to the elaborate palace.

Aided by British troops, who were subsequently commanded by the Duke of Wellington, the Spanish drove the French out of the Iberian Peninsula. At Tarifa, the enemy was defeated literally overnight in an offensive of 1811. What the world now knows as the Peninsular War (1808–1814) is in fact referred to in Spain as the War of Independence. During this troubled period, Spain's first, short-lived, constitution was drafted, and their colonies of South America won their independence.

Troubled Times

Ferdinand's return to the throne in 1814 destroyed any hopes left for a constitutional monarchy, while tension between liberals and conservatives led to a century of conflict, marked by the upheavals of the three Carlist wars and the abortive First Republic, which was proclaimed in 1873.

On the Andalucían coast, the 19th century was a time of tentative expansion. With piracy at an end, a number of towns and villages grew up along the shoreline, and the extension of the railway line to Almería in 1899 promoted the early development of the eastern region.

Alfonso XIII, just 16 years old, assumed the crown in 1902. Prosperity and stability continued to elude the country, which remained neutral during World War I. Against a murky background of violence, strikes, and regional strife, the king accepted the dictatorship of General Miguel Primo de Rivera in 1923. Seven years later, the opposition of radical forces toppled Primo de Rivera from power. Alfonso XIII went into exile following anti-royalist election results in 1931, and another republic was founded.

Parliamentary elections in 1933 resulted in a swing to the right, and public opinion became polarized. When the left came out on top in the elections of 1936, the situation deteriorated at an alarming rate. It came as no surprise when, six months later, General Francisco Franco led a large section of the army against the socialist government. Support for the Franco-led nationalist uprising came from monarchists, conservatives, and the right-wing Falangist organization, as well as the Roman Catholic Church, while liberals, socialists, Communists, and anarchists sided with the government.

The bloodshed lasted no less than three years and cost hundreds of thousands of lives. General Franco emerged as the leader of a shattered Spain. Many Republicans went into exile; others simply disappeared. The Republican mayor of Mijas caused a sensation when he finally surfaced in the 1960s after three decades in hiding — in his own home. Franco kept Spain out of World War II, despite Hitler's entreaties to the contrary. The Spanish nation gradually healed its wounds, though conditions in the country were difficult and life was far from easy.

Changing Fortunes

All that was to change, virtually overnight, as Spain's tourist potential began to be exploited in the 1950s. Credit was made available for the development of hotel complexes and apartment blocks, and former fishing villages like Torremolinos and Marbella began to change forever. Spain's admission to the United Nations in 1955, followed by the advent of jet travel and package holidays in the 1960s, subsequently opened up the coast to mass tourism.

With the death of General Franco in 1975, Spain returned to democracy. In accordance with Franco's wishes, the monarchy was restored in the person of King Juan Carlos, the grandson of Alfonso XIII (see page 20). More than just a figurehead, the king helped to thwart a military coup in 1981, keeping Spain firmly on a democratic course.

A process of decentralization was started, with more powers being devolved, although not equally, to 17 semiautonomous regions. As a consequence, on 28 February 1982, Andalucía was proclaimed an autonomous state. Also that year, the socialist government of Felipe González was elected and committed itself to Spain's successful integration into the European Community (EC), now known as the European

Union or EU. As a precondition of admission, the border with Gibraltar was reopened in February 1985, after a 16-year hiatus, and Spain was finally admitted to the EC in 1986. Despite high unemployment figures and separatist rumblings, the country's economy has remained one of the fastest growing in Western Europe.

King Juan Carlos became the monarch of Spain after General Franco's death.

Historical Landmarks

c.23,000b.c. Prehistoric man inhabits caves in southern Spain.

c.3000b.c. Iberian tribes migrate to Spain from North Africa.

1100b.c. Phoenicians found coastal settlements.

900b.c. Celts wander south from northern Europe.

650b.c. Greek traders found a series of colonies.

2nd century b.c. Romans conquer Spain.

a.d. 5th century Visigothic kingdom established.

711 Moors launch their conquest of Spain.

929 Caliphate of Córdoba founded.

11th–12th centuries The caliphate splinters into small kingdoms called taifas. Almoravid warriors move in (1086), followed by the Almohads (1151).

1212 Christians defeat Moors at Las Navas de Tolosa.

1232 Nasrid dynasty founded in Granada.

1492 Granada falls to Ferdinand and Isabella. Christopher Columbus discovers America.

16th century Emperor Charles V and King Philip II expand Spain's empire during the Golden Age.

1609 The moriscos are expelled from Spain.

1704 Great Britain captures Gibraltar.

1808 Napoleon sets his brother, Joseph, on the Spanish throne, triggering the War of Independence (1808–1814).

1902–31 Political unrest grows under King Alfonso XIII.

1936–39 Spanish Civil War.

1939–75 Dictatorship of General Francisco Franco.

1975 Spain returns to democracy. Monarchy restored. King Juan Carlos helps to thwart a military coup.

On 28 February, Andalucía is proclaimed an autonomous state.

Spain enters European Union (then European Economic Community).

1992 Sevilla hosts Expo '92.

WHERE TO GO

Most visitors to the Costa del Sol are based in one of the large coastal resorts to the west of Málaga (Torremolinos, Benalmádena, Fuengirola, Marbella or Estepona), while far fewer head east toward Nerja, Almuñécar, or even as far as Almería. Although the main aim for many is to relax on the beach and soak up as much sun as possible, increasing numbers arrive to play golf. It comes as little surprise, therefore, that the road signs proclaim the area west of Málaga not just the *Costa del Sol,* but the *Costa del Golf* also.

A few visitors forsake the beach for a day or two and venture out to either the amazingly varied historic towns and cities or the natural wonders of the national parks nearby. Málaga, Ronda, and perhaps Gibraltar can be seen in a day, but Sevilla, Córdoba, Granada, and the parks necessitate at least an overnight stop.

MÁLAGA

Málaga's international airport is the gateway to the Costa del Sol and Andalucía for most people. However, few visitors spend much time in the city itself. This is a shame, as Málaga is an ancient Andalucían city of not inconsiderable charm that offers a refreshing taste of the real Spain.

Founded by Phoenician traders more than 3,000 years ago, it came under Carthaginian and Roman rule before falling to the Moorish invasion force in 711. The Moors fortified the city, developing the settlement into a major trading port serving Granada, and it was one of the last cities in Spain to be re-conquered by Christian forces in 1487.

A good place to begin a tour is at Málaga's principle landmark, **Gibralfaro** (from the Arabic *Jebel al Faro*—Lighthouse Hill). Located some 130 m (425 ft) above the city, this

The tip-top of Gibralfaro offers a remarkable view of the cityscape below — though its no place for a midnight stroll.

hilltop is capped by the ramparts of a Phoenician castle reconstructed in the 14th century by the Moors (who went on to build the lighthouse that gave Gibralfaro its name). The restored walls and parapets offer a superb panoramic view of both the city below and the coastline disappearing into the horizon. Because it looks down on the Plaza de Toros, the hill also acts as free seating for bullfights taking place below. Although it is possible to walk here, it is not recommended. Not only is the pathway somewhat difficult in places, it is also a well-known hangout for muggers. Best, then, to take a taxi.

Back at sea level is the delightful **Paseo del Parque,** with contrasting fountains at either end, which connects the old town with the Plaza de Toros. On its south side, it is a lush seaside tropical garden enhanced by fountains, duck ponds, and small bars. The other side is home to the smaller Jardínes Puerta Oscura and two impressive buildings, the Ayuntamiento (Town Hall) and the 18th-century La Aduana (Old Custom House).

Immediately behind here is the sprawling **Alcazaba** fortress/palace complex that the Moors built between the 11th and 14th centuries. A cobbled path climbs up the hillside within the walls to the portal dubbed Arco del Cristo (Gateway of Christ). The victorious Christian army of Ferdinand and Isabella celebrated mass here when the fortress finally fell into their hands in 1487. Higher still, the one-time palace (a disappointment compared with those in Granada and Sevilla) contains a small archaeological museum. Beside the entrance to

Finding Your Way Around

alcázar	fortress	**jardín**	garden
iglesia	church	**mercado**	market
mezquita	mosque	**isla**	island
ascensor	lift, elevator	**muelle**	docks
autopista	motorway	**murallas**	ramparts
camino	highway	**museo**	museum
avenida	avenue	**oficina de**	tourist
ayuntamiento	town hall	**turismo**	office
barrio	quarter	**paseo**	boulevard
cabo	cape	**playa**	beach
calle	street	**plaza**	square
carretera	road	**plaza de**	bullring
castillo	castle	**toros**	
ciudad vieja	old town	**puerto**	harbor
correos	post office	**río**	river
cueva	cave	**vía**	avenue
estación de	railway	**sierra**	mountain
ferrocarril			range
faro	lighthouse	**derecha**	right
fortaleza	fortress	**izquierda**	left
todo derecho	straight ahead		

the Alcazaba are the partially excavated ruins of a Roman theater, the only visible remains of the ancient city.

A short walk away is the **cathedral,** known locally as La Manquita — the one-armed lady — because one of its twin towers remains unfinished. The north tower soars 100 m (some 330 ft) above the street, but work on the other, a forlorn stump of stone, stopped in 1783 because of a lack of money.

Málaga was the birthplace of Pablo Ruiz Picasso, though the young artist left his native city at age 14 for the more cosmopolitan climates of Madrid and Barcelona. The house he was born in, **Casa**

Dubbed La Manquita by locals, the cathedral's north tower soars over Málaga.

Natal Picasso at Plaza de la Merced 14, doubles as a small museum and research center. On a larger scale is the nearby **Museo de Bellas Artes** (Fine Arts Museum), an old Renaissance-style palace with pleasing patios. In late 1999, it was being converted into the future **Museo Picasso** (Picasso Museum).

The **Museo de Artes y Tradiciones Populares** on the western edge of the old town is easily missed, but that would be a mistake. Situated in the Posada de la Victoria, a charming early 17th-century historic inn that is incongruous with its surroundings, the museum offers a fascinating glimpse of how life was lived in Málaga in generations past.

On the way back to the center of Málaga, stop for a moment or two at the century-old **Mercado Atarazanas** (market). Each morning it is filled with women admiring the bountiful displays of meat, fish, fruit, and vegetables, and shopping in the traditional manner for fresh, not plastic-wrapped, produce. This is also the western boundary of a collection of small roads and pedestrian-only streets that end at the main street, Calle Marqués de Larios, and combine to form Málaga's principal shopping center. You can buy almost anything here, from foodstuffs to footwear, but be advised that the siesta still reigns in this part of Spain and nothing is open between about 2pm and 5pm.

NORTH OF MÁLAGA

Just an hour's drive north of Málaga lies some magnificent mountain scenery. The national park of **El Torcal de**

The Old World bustle of the Mercado Atarazanas—prepackaged produce and TV dinners have no home here!

Antequera is a high limestone plateau that has been eroded by rainwater into a fantasy landscape of fluted pinnacles and towers. Hikers can explore the marked trails, which are up to 5 km (3 miles) in length and wind among the rocks, and enjoy panoramic views back to Málaga and the distant blue Mediterranean. This is where you will also find a most wonderful small hotel, La Posada del Torcal.

Near the town of Alora, you will find the breathtaking gorge known as the **Garganta del Chorro.** Three hundred meters (1,000 feet) in depth, this sheer-sided canyon is cut by the Guadalhorce River. It is also accessible from Málaga by train; ask for a ticket to El Chorro. An improbable concrete catwalk called the Camino del Rey (The King's Way) crosses a vertical cliff and continues into the heart of the gorge, a dizzying 65 m (200 ft) above the river. It was built in the 1920s to provide access for workers digging tunnels for a hydroelectricity project. The artificial dams above the gorge have created attractive lakes, known as the **Pantanos del Chorro.** Fringed with woods, sandy beaches, and campsites, they constitute a refreshing change of scenery from the heat and bustle of the coast.

WEST OF MÁLAGA

Some of the world's most popular beach resorts line the coast that stretches 162 km (100 miles) to the Rock of Gibraltar.

Torremolinos

Just a few kilometers west of Málaga's international airport is Torremolinos. In the late 1950s and early 1960s, it was the first resort on the Costa del Sol to establish a reputation as a popular international playground. Although little more than an overgrown village, it was a haven for young northern Europeans seeking an inexpensive vacation with much

Built on a reputation as a popular international playground, the beach at Torremolinos lives up to the legend.

sun, sand, and sangría. Since then, it has built, quite literally, on that reputation. And although it is nowhere as inexpensive, even relatively, as it once was, it is still a highly popular tourist destination.

Wall-to-wall hotels and apartments reach way back from the beaches and there's no denying that it delivers everything sun-hungry vacationers could wish for. Its miles of glorious beaches, guaranteed sun, cheap alcohol and food, numerous bars, discotheques, and nightclubs attract a clientele that is largely British, although other northern European countries are still well represented here. (Even a fair number of Americans and Russians are now visiting.) This cosmopolitan, but not by any means sophisticated, international invasion has completely overwhelmed the town. There can be few places in the world where foreign languages, principally English, are more dominant than the native language. But that is certainly the case in Torremolinos.

Although the first mention of the town dates back to 1498, there is really nothing here of historical significance. The town itself, especially **Calle San Miguel,** is simply a profusion of shops. At the bottom of San Miguel a series of winding stairways, lined by shops of course, lead down towards a 7 km (nearly 5 mile) sweep of golden coastline. This consists of six beaches connected by the wonderful Paseo Maritimo (beach promenade) and broken only by the rocky promontory of Castillo de Santa Clara, which separates the Bajondillo (east) and Carihuela (west) sections of town.

Chiringuitos (small beachside restaurants) are in plentiful supply, especially in the former fishing village of **La Carihuela.** There are still a few bona fide fishermen about, and if you can manage to drag yourself out of bed between six and eight in the morning, you'll see them returning to shore in their gaily painted, flat-bottomed wooden boats, with nets of sardines and anchovies. At lunchtime, you can sample the morning's catch, skewered on a wooden stick and grilled over a fire on the beach (see page 97).

Many other popular attractions lie close at hand, including the wave pools and water slides of Atlantis Aquapark, the horse show at the Club El Rancho, and the 18-hole course of the nearby

Attention all shoppers — Calle San Miguel is well-worth part of an afternoon.

Parador del Golf. But the biggest draw in Torremolinos continues to be the bars, discos, and clubs that have earned the resort its international reputation for non-stop nightlife.

Benalmádena-Costa

Heading west it appears, at first glance, that Benalmádena-Costa is indistinguishable from its close neighbor. However, this isn't really so. In fact, it is somewhat less built up and frenetic than Torremolinos, even though it is well endowed with bars, discos, and clubs. Its fine beaches stretch for 9 km (over 5 miles), beginning at the large and attractive Puerto Deportivo on the border with Torremolinos. Focal points are the three Moorish watch towers; the pink, neo-Moorish walls

---

Costa del Sol Highlights

Marbella Old Town: Centered on its old church tower, a maze of narrow streets filled with little shops and cafés.

Gibraltar: The Rock of Gibraltar, a British colony since 1713, has several famous sights—the Apes' Den, Upper Galleries, and views across the Strait of Gibraltar to the coast of Morocco.

Ronda: A fortified hilltop town divided by the spectacular Tajo gorge and linked by an 18th-century bridge. There are many walking paths in the area.

Sevilla: Capital of Andalucía, with a fine Gothic cathedral, Moorish Alcázar, and historic Barrio Santa Cruz district. Home of flamenco, bullfighting, and the colorful Fería de Abril.

Córdoba: Formerly a Moorish capital, this is one of the medieval world's most important cities; famous for its mosque, La Mezquita.

Granada: Home of the magnificent hilltop Alhambra Palace, in a wonderful setting at the foot of the Sierra Nevada Mountains.

Benalmádena-Costa has a glamorous modern casino—
quite a contrast to the ancient Moorish watch towers.

of **Castillo El Bil-Bil,** built by a Frenchwoman in the 1930s
and used for concerts, exhibitions, and as a tourist office; and
one of the Costa del Sol's casinos at the huge and impressive
Torrequebrada complex.

A couple of kilometers (about a mile) inland and high
above the sea lies the village of Benalmádena-Pueblo. Its
Museo Arqueológico y de Arte Colombino is an institution
of national importance. The museum takes pride in its collection of Pre-Columbian art (said to be the most important
of its kind in Spain), with jewelry, statuary, and ceramics
from all the major cultures. Also in the Benalmádena area is
the Tívoli World amusement park, in the suburb of Arroyo de
la Miel (see page 91), the Sea Life aquarium in the Puerto
Deportivo, and the Eagle Park at the Colomares Castle.

Fuengirola

Nine kilometers (6 miles) down the line is Fuengirola, another resort that's hugely popular with the British. Here, bacon and eggs, fish and chips, darts, snooker, English beer, and bars showing English soccer games are the norm. But Fuengirola has assimilated this without losing its Spanish character. And this is particularly true in early October during the annual fair, when the town becomes a blaze of color and noise, and most every man, woman, and child dons typical Andalucían dress. Tradition survives, too, as the commercial fishing fleet is an ongoing concern.

The Plaza de la Constitución in the town center has numerous pleasant cafés lining the square beneath the

Gather with friends or make some new ones on one of Fuengirola's beachfront restaurant patios.

church bell tower, and nearby is the bullring and the small **Zoo Municipal.** Across the river at the western end of town rise the remains of the **Castillo de Sohail.** Abd-er-Rahman III built this hilltop fortress in the 10th century and gradually a settlement grew up around the walls. Taken by the Christians in a bloody battle in 1487, Sohail was then leveled on the orders of the "Catholic kings." After it was rebuilt, it was occupied by French troops during the Peninsular War, who left behind a souvenir of their stay — the cannons that are now displayed along the promenade of the **Paseo Marítimo.** Other attractions here include a variety of water sports, a marina, the fishing harbor, a sailing school, the waterslides of the Mijas Aqua Park, the El Cartujano horse show, and horse racing at the newly opened Mijas Hippodrome.

Mijas

Eight kilometers (5 miles) inland from Fuengirola and clinging to the hillside is **Mijas.** Surrounded by modern villas and *urbanizaciones* (developments), it looks from the outside like any other quaint village with whitewashed houses. But Mijas is different. Most of the houses have been converted into upscale shops, restaurants, or bars, making the village itself a unique tourist attraction. Traffic is banned from the center, so if you don't feel like the short walk from the parking lot, take a mule taxi.

Mijas has Spain's only square **bullring,** and across from it, beautifully tended gardens slope down to a cliff-top mirador, with fine views all along the coast. There is another mirador beside the car park. On one side of this natural balcony you will find a tiny **chapel** dedicated to the Virgen de la Peña (Our Lady of the Mountain), set in a grotto carved from living rock.

Marbella

Sheltered by the mountains of the Sierra Blanca on one side and with the Mediterranean Sea on the other, Marbella has earned a reputation for being the most aristocratic of Costa del Sol's resorts. This began in the 1950s when Prince Alfonso von Hohenlohe bought land and built himself a luxurious home here. It became so popular with his guests that he developed it into the Marbella Club Hotel, and that in turn launched Marbella as a trendy gathering place for the jet set in the 1960s. Today the town is a playground for the rich and famous, frequented by celebrities and politicians, royalty and business tycoons. As a consequence, this has seen the further development, both here and along the coast, of the largest collection of luxury hotels in Spain. Naturally, then, prices are much higher here than in the other coastal resorts, but you get what you pay for in terms of superior standards of accommodation, service, and cuisine.

Marbella is certainly a town of two parts. The largest, by far, is the modern section and the center of this, clustered around the palm trees and fountains of the Parque de la Alameda, is taken up with busy sidewalk cafés, smart boutiques, banks, and real estate agents' offices. The construction of a four-lane bypass has happily put an end to the crush of traffic that regularly used to jam this part of town. It is at its most attractive, though, by the sea, where the municipality of Marbella encompasses some 28 km (17 miles) of beachfront. The promenade winds along the beaches of El Fuerte and Fontanilla, passing a **marina** (*Puerto Deportivo*) with moorings for several hundred pleasure boats, overlooked by the tall spire of the lighthouse. Some lively beach bars and restaurants make this a popular part of town.

The promenade extends west for a mile or two, between attractive apartment complexes and long stretches of golden sands. The monuments of modern Marbella cling to the hills on the western outskirts. The King of Saudi Arabia's holiday home —it looks like the White House in Washington, D.C., only slightly larger— hides behind a row of pines and palms on a hilltop just above the highway, surrounded by high security fences. On a neighboring rise stands Marbella's modern-style mosque, the Mezquita del Rey Abdulaziz Al Saud, which is open to the public every afternoon except Friday.

The luxury hotels of Marbella line the promenade and are never far from the beach.

But Marbella has its historic side, too. In fact, its history dates back some 1,600 years, even though most of what can be seen, in the town at least, dates from the time of the Catholic Monarchs and later. North of the main road, the **Casco Antiguo** (Old Town) provides an intriguing glimpse of the past that has been cleverly integrated to cater to modern visitors. First, sit at a café table in the **Plaza de los Naranjos** (Square of the Orange Trees), where you can admire the noble 16th-century façade of the **Casa Consistorial** (Town Hall) and soak up the atmosphere. Then wander through the maze of narrow, twisting streets where the whitewashed walls are decorated with colorful baskets of flowers.

As you explore the neighborhood, you'll come across the historic parish church with its landmark bell tower, and the convents of La Trinidad and San Francisco (it is said that Miguel de Cervantes, creator of the famous Don Quixote, lodged at the latter). Uphill from the church lie the crumbling walls of the Moorish *castillo*. Scattered throughout this area also are an eclectic array of shops and galleries.

Other places of interest in Marbella are the Bonsai Museum, the only one in Spain and one of the best in the world, and the Museum of Spanish Contemporary Engravings. Housed in a structure important in its own right, the latter is the first of its kind in Spain and has works by Picasso, Miró, Tapies, and other such famous artists.

Just outside of Marbella are three other places with ancient

historic connections: the Roman Villa mosaics dating from the first and second centuries at Río Verde near the beach; the Paleo-Christian basilica Vega del Mar in San Pedro de Alcántara; and the Las Bovedas (The Cellars) Roman baths at Guadalmina.

With the increasing popularity of Marbella, high society has moved west to the chic suburb of Nueva Andalu-

Dress respectfully when you visit the Mezquita del Rey Abdulaziz.

Sightseeing Essentials

Sevilla: **Cathedral and Giralda**, Plaza Virgen de los Reyes; Tel. (95) 421 49 71. Mon–Sat 11am–5pm, Sun 2pm–6pm. Admission: 750 ptas (€4.51), free on Sun. **Real Alcázar**, Plaza del Triunfo; Tel. (95) 450 23 23. Tues–Sat 9:30am–8pm, Sun and holidays 9:30am–6pm, closed Mon. Admission: 700 ptas (€4.21). **Museo de Bellas Artes**, Plaza del Museo, 9; Tel. (95) 422 07 90. Tues 3pm–8pm, Wed–Sat 9am–8pm, Sun 9am–3pm, closed Mon. Admission: 250 ptas (€1.50). **Torre del Oro**, Paseo de las Delicias; Tel. (95) 422 24 19. Tues–Fri 10am–2pm, Sat, Sun and holidays 11am–2pm, closed Mon. Admission: 100 ptas (€0.60), free Tues. **Plaza de Toros**, Paseo Colón, 12; Tel. (95) 422 45 77. Mon-Sun 9:30am-2pm and 3pm-6pm. Admission: 250 ptas (€1.50). **Casa de Pilatos**, Plaza de Pilatos, s/n; Tel. (95) 422 52 98. Mon-Sun 9am-7:30pm. Admission: 1000 ptas (€6.01).

Córdoba: **Mezquita/Cathedral**, c/. Cardenal Herrero, 1; Tel. (957) 47 05 12. Mon–Sat 10am–7pm, Sun and holidays 2pm–7pm. Admission: 750 ptas (€4.51). **Alcázar de los Reyes Cristianos**, c/. Caballerizas Reales, s/n; Tel. (957) 42 01 51. Tues–Sat 10am–2pm and 6pm–8pm, Sun and holidays 9:30am–3pm, closed Mon. Admission: 300 ptas (€1.80). **Conjunto Arqueológico Medina Azahara**, Ctra. Palma del Río; Tel. (957) 32 91 30. Tues–Sat 10am–2pm and 6pm–8:30pm, Sun and holidays 10am–2pm, closed Mon. Admission: 250 ptas (€1.50), European Union citizens free.

Granada: Alhambra and Generalife, Tel. (958) 22 75 27. Open daily 8:30am–5pm, night visits 8pm–10pm. Admission: 675 ptas (€4.06), Sun free. **Capilla Real**, c/. Oficios; Tel. (958) 22 92 39. Mon–Sat 10:30am–1pm and 3:30pm–6pm, Sun 10am–1pm and 3:30pm–6:30pm. Admission: 200 ptas (€1.20). **Cathedral**, Gran Vía de Colón; Tel. (958) 22 29 59. Open daily 10:30am–1pm and 4pm–7:30pm. Admission: 200 ptas (€1.20).

cía, and its magnificent harbor, **Puerto Banús.** Sleek, unbelievably expensive yachts line the quayside, and Bentleys, Porsches, Rolls Royces, and Mercedes adorn the streets. There's a glamorous line-up of expensive restaurants and high-class boutiques that seem to be permanently open. High rollers haunt the tables in the nearby Casino Marbella, then sip martinis and watch the sun rise from the decks of their luxury yachts. Even if you can't quite afford to join in, it's fun just to watch how the other half lives. The aquarium in Peurto Banús may be small, but it is interesting nonetheless.

This part of the Costa del Sol is also a golfer's paradise. In 1999, nearly 30 golf clubs were in operation between Málaga and Sotogrande. These courses cater to all levels, from beginners to experts taking part in the most important competitions in the golf world's calendar. At least half a

Scope out the yachts that fill the harbor at Puerto Banús — they may allow for a glimpse of the rich and famous.

dozen quality courses can be found between the western edge of Marbella and San Pedro de Alcántara.

Ojén

Inland from Marbella lie the high peaks of the Sierra Blanca, the most distinctive being La Concha (The Seashell), which rises directly above the town. A scenic road leads to the village of Ojén (famous for its *aguardiente,* a kind of brandy once produced here) and on to the mountain pass called Puerto de Ojén. Just beyond, a road on the left leads to the Refugio de Juanar, a hunting lodge set at the heart of a large national game reserve. The peace and tranquility found here has attracted numerous famous personalities. Not least of these is General Charles de Gaulle of France, who finished his memoirs here in 1970. This is the haunt of mountain hare, partridge, and the ibex (Capra pyrenaica), a wild mountain goat with large horns that is unique to Spain.

Estepona

This is the last major resort town on the western part of the Costa del Sol, and it provides all the vacation essentials—good beaches, golf courses, restaurants, and a marina—in a small-town atmosphere. Low-rise apartment blocks, unpretentious restaurants, and hotels overlook the palm-lined **Paseo Marítimo,** a promenade furnished with park benches, flower displays, and a little playground.

Originally a Roman settlement, Estepona preserves the remains of Moorish fortifications and watchtowers, an 18th-century parish church, and an expressionistic bullring, a startling piece of modern architecture which is beginning to look rather worse for wear. On either side of the town itself, gracious and upscale hotel resorts are beginning to make an emblematic impression on the coastline.

The pristine white walls of the Pueblos Blancos are capped by red rooftops.

Beyond Estepona, development is more sporadic, though there are some luxury resorts at Sotogrande and Puerto Duquesa. About 6 km (4 miles) outside of town, a mountain road takes you up to **Casares,** a spectacular white hilltop village clinging precariously to the rugged slopes below its Moorish fort. The road commands sweeping views of the coast and countryside, and on a clear day the eye is inevitably drawn to the twin peaks flanking the Strait of Gibraltar—the Rock of Gibraltar on the right, and Morocco's Jebel Musa on the left. These were known to the ancients as the Pillars of Hercules, and in ancient times marked the limits of the known world.

Toward Gibraltar

Gibraltar looms ever larger as you approach **San Roque,** which was established by Spanish refugees who fled the Rock when the English captured it in 1704. Building blocks for the town were found, conveniently, in the nearby ruins of Roman Carteya; today, though, little remains of the classical site. Branch off the N-340 here and head for La Línea de la Concepción and the Rock itself. **La Línea** has experienced a mini-boom since the border with Gibraltar was reopened in 1985 after a blockade lasting 16 years, but is still a dreary place.

It has been ascertained that Gibraltar was a home for prehistoric man. Neanderthal skulls were found in 1848 and 1928, and Gibraltar is considered one of the final bastions for this species. Although it is known that the Phoenicians, Greeks, and Carthaginians were aware of Gibraltar, and that the Romans ruled here from about 500 B.C. to A.D. 475, no town was ever built. The Visigoths and Vandals destroyed almost all traces of culture in the area, and it wasn't until after the Moors invaded, in 711, that the first city was constructed. However, even that wasn't until nearly 450 years later in 1160.

Entering Gibraltar

If you arrive by car (**Gibraltar** is only two hours' drive from Málaga), you have two choices, neither of which is ideal. It is easier, and often much faster, to leave the car in one of the parking lots in La Linea and cross the border on foot. Once in Gibraltar, a car is a hindrance in the town center, and only really useful if you want to take a tour of the Upper Rock. However, the downside of this strategy is the possibility, too high for comfort, of having your car broken into in La Linea.

If you want to take your car with you, bear in mind that every now and again, and too frequently at that, you may be subject to long delays in either direction. The Spanish authorities, in their ongoing battle with Great Britain over the sovereignty of Gibraltar, have decided to make the normally minimal border formalities long and drawn out by checking everything and everyone. Either way, beyond the customs area, entrance to Gibraltar is across the middle of the airport runway, then past the defensive walls to the town center.

The next three centuries saw numerous battles, and it wasn't until 1462 that Gibraltar was finally re-conquered by the Spanish. In the early 18th century, problems over succession to the Spanish throne led to an Anglo-Dutch force capturing Gibraltar in 1704. That led in 1713 to the treaty of Utrecht under which Spain ceded its rights to Gibraltar to the British. However, the Spanish didn't give up without a fight—more than one, actually. In 1727, they failed in a siege, and in 1779 combined Spanish and French forces totaling 50,000 laid the final Great Siege against just 5,000 defenders. After four years of much hardship, the siege ended in 1783. It wasn't until 1830 that Gibraltar achieved the status of a British crown colony, which it holds to this day.

The town and harbor lie on the east slope of the Rock, overlooking the bay, with the narrow defile of **Main Street** cutting through the middle. This is lined with duty-free shops selling liquor, perfume, cameras, CD players, video recorders, and electronic goods and British-style pubs serving pints of beer and bar lunches. The unit of currency is the Gibraltarian pound (equal to the British pound), but shops and other businesses accept pounds sterling and pesetas as well.

Also at sea level is the **Gibraltar Museum,** housed in a building containing what are considered the best preserved Moorish baths in Europe. The museum has interesting exhibits on Gibraltar's history. Of interest, too, is **Nelson's Anchorage,** where Admiral Nelson's body is said to have been brought in a barrel of rum after the Battle of Trafalgar on 21 October 1805, and the nearby 100-ton Victorian supergun, the largest gun of its type in the world.

Main Street ends at the Referendum Gates. Beyond lies the **cable-car station,** where you can take a trip to the top of the Rock with a stop halfway to visit the **Apes' Den.** The tail-less Barbary apes that inhabit the Rock are natives of

Get a piece of the Rock—it's no wonder that the European powers have all fought to possess the mighty Gibraltar.

North Africa, descended from monkeys brought over by sailors as pets and ships' mascots. Legend has it that if the apes ever leave the Rock, then British rule will come to an end. When the apes' population declined significantly during World War II, Winston Churchill himself was worried, and the monkeys have been on special rations ever since. The views from the summit 426 m (396 ft) up are spectacular, particularly across the strait to Morocco, along the coast toward Estepona, and down the sheer east face of the Rock to the water holding areas (for desalination) and the beaches of Sandy Bay, Catalan Bay, and Eastern Beach.

Whether you're traveling in your own car or in an official taxi or minivan, don't leave Gibraltar without taking a tour of the **Upper Rock Nature Reserve** area. On the way up note the yellow patches and their accompanying metal rings; these were used when manually hauling the heavy cannons up the Rock. Also of interest is the fact that there is no soil on the Upper Rock; the 600 species of wildflower here grow directly out of the limestone from which the Rock is formed.

First stop is **Saint Michael's Cave,** an impressive natural grotto that is sometimes used as a venue for musical performances. Then stop to see the apes, and at the north end of the Rock, take time to explore the **Upper Galleries.** These are a system of tunnels blasted through the inside of the rock face during the Great Siege of the late 18th century. Note that the cannon emplacements slope downward, a clever innovation that allowed the defenders to fire directly at the Spanish/French forces attacking from La Linea. What cannot be seen is the 51 km (32 miles) of tunnels that were excavated during World War II, and it is from these that General Eisenhower conducted the Allied invasion of North Africa. On the way back to the town lies the **Moorish castle,** which apart from its 14th-century tower is of little interest.

The Battle of Trafalgar

Fifty kilometers (30 miles) northwest of Tarifa lies the Cabo de Trafalgar (from the Arabic Tarif al-Gar, or Cape of the Cave). Off this headland on 21 October 1805, a British fleet of 27 ships under Admiral Horatio Nelson engaged a combined French and Spanish fleet of 33 ships in one of history's most famous naval battles, which established Britain's naval supremacy for the next 100 years. At the end of the day, the enemy was routed, losing nearly two-thirds of its ships. No British vessels were lost, but Nelson was hit by a sniper's bullet, and died just before the battle's end.

Algeciras

Just across the bay from Gibraltar is an uninspiring port town whose only saving grace, on good days at least, is its unsurpassed views of Gibraltar. From the harbor, hydrofoils and car ferries cross the strait to Ceuta, a Spanish protectorate, and to Tangier in Morocco. A day trip to Ceuta is certainly possible, but there is not much, beyond shopping, of interest there. Much more interesting and exciting is to continue on about 25 miles to Tetuan, Morocco, parts of which seem to have remained unchanged for centuries. Because of the two-hour time difference between Ceuta and Morocco, it's dif-

The sea will always be the main attraction of Costa del Sol—it's difficult to resist.

ficult, but possible, to see in one day. Therefore, an overnight stop in Ceuta is recommended. For additional information, see the *Berlitz Travel Guide to Morocco*.

Tarifa

This is where the waters of the Mediterranean mingle with those of the Atlantic, and bring the Costa del Sol to an end. Europe looks across the Strait of Gibraltar to Africa, with the Rif Mountains of Morocco dominating the horizon a mere 13 km (8 miles) away. A section of the old Moorish walls remains, as does the 10th century fortress. However, it is not its history that attracts most visitors these days. The beaches stretching to the west are a mecca for windsurfers. The prevailing wind, known as the *Poniente,* is from the west, making the beaches among the windiest in Europe.

The windsurfers are not the only ones to take advantage of the reliable breeze; the hillsides above the town have sprouted a veritable forest of wind-powered electricity generators. In spring and autumn, storks, buzzards, and other soaring birds fill the skies as they climb in the rising thermals before gliding across the strait on their annual migration, congregating here where the sea crossing is at its shortest.

EAST OF MÁLAGA

The eastern part of the Costa del Sol stretches for more than 200 km (125 miles) from Málaga to Almería. This part of the coast has a different feel from the western section, with less intensive development and, in parts, a much rockier and attractive shoreline.

Málaga to Nerja

Leaving the suburbs of Málaga, you arrive immediately in **Rincón de la Victoria,** a Spanish resort largely given over to weekend apartments owned by the local city dwellers. But prehistoric man was here first, occupying a cave on the Málaga side of the town known as **Cueva del Tesoro** (Treasure Cave). Cave paintings and prehistoric remains, including a shrine to the goddess Noctiluca, have been found and there is a beautiful underground lake with stalactites. According to legend, five Moorish kings buried a huge treasure inside the cave, but it has never been found.

Torre del Mar is the gateway to the wine and raisin-producing region of the Axarquía, and its capital, **Vélez-Má-**

laga, which lies 4 km (2 ½ miles) inland. Founded by the Phoenicians, Vélez sprawls around a historic center dominated by a Moorish *alcazaba* and two venerable churches: the late-Gothic Iglesia de San Juan Bautista and the Iglesia de Santa María (which incorporates a section of the town's former mosque).

In the village of **Torrox-Costa,** as elsewhere on the eastern Costa, self-catering accommodations predominate over hotels. Once dedicated to fishing and agriculture, **Torrox-Costa** is now an expanding resort with extensive Roman ruins.

Nerja

Nerja is the one large international resort to the east of Málaga, and it's a popular destination for British, German, and Scandinavian vacationers. The town is smaller than the resort towns in the west, and despite the intensive development in the hills surrounding it, has also managed to retain some of its village atmosphere. The nightlife is lively, though quieter than in Torremolinos, and the beaches are prettier, if smaller. (They're tucked into rocky coves.)

The area also offers good opportunities for hiking, horseback riding, scuba diving, snorkeling, and an-

The Balcón de Europa is a hot spot, although it sits precariously on the rocks.

The interesting sculptures at Cuerva de Nerja accompany the natural rock formations.

gling, giving Nerja the edge for those seeking a more active vacation.

Hotels and restaurants cluster around the **Balcón de Europa,** a palm-fringed clifftop promenade jutting out over the sea, dividing the sandy crescent of La Caletilla beach on the west from La Calahonda on the east.

Just 6 km (4 miles) east of the beach of **Maro** is the famous **Cueva de Nerja** (Cave of Nerja). This huge cavern was discovered in 1959 when a group of local boys stumbled on it one day while they were out hunting bats. Floodlights illuminate the impressive limestone formations, including a stalagmite/stalactite over 32 m (105 ft) high and 18 m (59 ft) in diameter. On display are archaeological remains confirming that these caves were inhabited 30,000 years ago. The Nerja Festival of Music and Dance, held in early July, takes place in the acoustically acclaimed Sala de la Cascada. Nearby a rather attractive aqueduct stands as testimony to the creative skills of the region's earlier generations.

Inland from Nerja, the corrugated hills of the Sierra de Tejeda rise up toward the village of **Frigiliana.** Under the Moors, it was one of the many prosperous villages within the Kingdom of Granada. Today, the historic center is regarded as one of the most outstanding examples of Moorish village architecture on the Costa del Sol, with a lovely 16th-century church and ruined Moorish castle.

The Far East

After Nerja, the scenery changes dramatically; the mountains begin to cascade to the sea and the panoramas of the ragged coastline are magnificent. Just before La Herradura, a rather neat little town with a nice beach, road signs proclaim that you are now in the Provincia de Granada. Until you pass into Almería, this part of the Costa del Sol, the most attractive but least known, is now officially called the Costa Tropical.

Almuñécar is the first town of any size, and has an ancient history. A fine **aqueduct** stands as a monument to the skills of the Roman engineers who constructed it during the reign of Antoninus Pius in the second century A.D. A port for Granada in Moorish times, Almuñécar continued to enjoy a certain prestige after the Reconquest when Juan de Herrera, the architect of El Escorial, Philip II's grand monastery cum palace near Madrid, was commissioned to design the parish church. These days the town, set around an attractive curving beach, is an increasingly popular family resort.

Along the road from Almuñécar, pretty villas with spectacular coastal views dot the hillsides until, all of a sudden, the scenery changes dramatically. As the coast flattens out, a town of whitewashed houses atop a rocky, cone-shaped hill comes into view. Called **Salobreña,** it makes for an impressive sight. A Moorish castle, beautifully restored, stands isolated at the heart of the village.

Salobreña stands as the gateway to the agriculturally rich *vega* (plain) of the thriving port city of **Motril.** Sugarcane, the source of the greenery, flourishes here. The sugar refineries in the area have earned the town its nickname—Little

Crops of sugarcane make postage stamps of yellow and green that frame the pretty village of Salobreña.

Cuba. Like that country, Motril is known for its rum, although its residents are crafty enough to make just about enough for local consumption, and no more. Motril and Salobreña have their own extensive beaches and there are many more to come as the road continues eastward.

The next 40 km (25 miles) is a conservation area and the least developed of any section of the Costa del Sol. The small towns and villages, reminiscent of what the rest of the coastline used to be like before the mass tourist invasion, have a very limited supply of hotels, which means that even in midsummer, the beaches are far from overcrowded. What's more, it's possible to be swimming in the Mediterranean while the snow-covered peaks of the Sierra Nevada shimmer in the distance.

This scenery changes, and much for the worse, after **Adra,** an important fishing and fish processing center. The N-340 crosses a vast and dreary plain where every available piece of level land has been covered by ugly plastic green-houses that produce much of Europe's winter vegetables. The road rejoins the coast at **Aguadulce** where tourists, mainly Spanish, enjoy good beaches, new golf courses, and marinas. Here, the mountains meet the sea again, and the journey onto Almería is short but attractive.

Almería

Rich in history, **Almería** was once the most important city in Moorish Spain. The Almería of today is a pleasant provincial capital that's worth a visit if your travels take you to the east-ern limits of the Costa del Sol.

There are only two major sights. Abd-er-Rahman III's massive **Alcazaba** looms large on the hilltop above the city. Although an earthquake caused extensive damage in 1522, the crenellated ocher outer walls and a section of the turret-ed ramparts stand firm, providing wide-ranging vistas over the city and the sea. And the forbidding, fortified **cathedral** that stands just inland from the waterfront Paseo de Almería was built during the 16th century, when Barbary pirates were terrorizing the coast (see page 18).

Inland from Almería lies one of the most un-European landscapes on the European continent. The **Sierra de Alhamilla** is a desert of barren mountains, rocky ravines, and dry gravel riverbeds; spiky agave plants and prickly pears are the only vegetation. The region's uncanny resemblance to the American West made it a popular film location for spaghetti westerns, including such classics as *A Fistful of Dollars* and *The Good, the Bad, and the Ugly*, which set a young Clint Eastwood on the road to stardom in Hollywood. Near the vil-

Beware—after dark the Alcazaba in Almería tends to be a favorite of thieves.

lage of Tabernas is an area known as **Mini-Hollywood,** where two spaghetti-western film sets have been preserved as tourist attractions, complete with horses, cowboys, and barroom brawls.

INLAND EXCURSIONS

For a complete contrast to the sun, sea, and sangría atmosphere of the coast, you need only drive inland for a few hours to reach the cultural, historical, and architectural attractions of Ronda, Jerez de la Frontera, Sevilla, Córdoba and Granada—the great cities of Andalucía. If your time is limited, try one of the day trips offered in all the major resorts or focus your attention on Ronda. Most of the other destinations require an overnight stay.

Ronda

The opening of an improved road from San Pedro de Alcántara to Ronda has ended the isolation of this mountain area, and shortened the driving time from the coast to an hour. One of the most spectacularly situated towns in Europe, Ronda sits atop a cliff-bound plateau, cleaved through the middle by a sheer-sided gorge. The older, Moorish part of town (La Ciudad) lies to the south of the ravine, linked by an 18th-century bridge to El Mercadillo, the modern district that arose after the Reconquista.

The gorge, known as **El Tajo,** is a deep and narrow crevasse that plunges 150 m (490 ft) to the foaming Río Guadalevín, a tributary of the Guadiaro River. During the Civil War, nationalist sympathizers in the town were hurled to their deaths in the gorge, an event recalled by Hemingway in his novel *For Whom the Bell Tolls.* You can enjoy a superb view of the Tajo and the patchwork of fields beyond from the **Puente Nuevo** (New Bridge), built in 1788, as well as from the walkways that follow the edge of the gorge.

Cross the bridge into the **Ciudad,** the old Moorish enclave which remained impervious to Christian assault until 1485, to see most of Ronda's most important monuments. On one side of the Plaza de Campillo square stands the **Palacio de Mondragón,** constructed by Abomelic, King of Ronda, in 1314 and later taken over by the Christian conquerors. A Renaissance portal, a distinguished later addition, opens onto spacious court-yards where horseshoe arches, Arabic inscriptions, and dis-tinctive tile ornaments indi-cate the Moorish origins of this grand building.

A block or so away, Ron-da's original mosque survives in the form of the **Church of Santa María la Mayor.** The minaret was converted into a bell tower, and a Gothic nave was tacked on to the original structure, followed by a high altar in ornate 16th-century

Ernest Hemingway immor-talized the gory history of El Tajo in a popular novel.

Better to see a bullring without the bull? Some people would rather skip the thrill (or chill) of the fight.

Plateresque style, and some finely carved Baroque choir stalls. The church overlooks the Plaza de la Duquesa de Parcent, the main square, with the long, elegant façade of the Ayuntamiento (Town Hall) gracing another side.

Heading back toward the Puente Nuevo, stop to view the exterior of the **Palacio del Marqués de Salvatierra,** an 18th-century Renaissance mansion famous for its wrought-iron balconies made in the traditional Ronda style. Note, also, the carved stone figures above the entrance. Nearby stands **La Casa del Rey Moro** (The Moorish King's House), which is a curious combination of the water mine and gardens designed by the French landscaper Jean Claude Nicolas Forestier in the 1920s. Beyond here the road curves down toward the Tajo, where two more bridges—the **Puente Viejo** (Old Bridge) built in 1616 on top of Roman foundations and the Moorish **Puente Arabe**—span the gorge and offer striking views of the chasm. Down by the river stands the **Baños Árabes** (Moorish Baths), with the vaulted roof still intact.

Immediately back across the Puente Nuevo, a Parador hotel occupies what was the old Town Hall, and just beyond that is Ronda's Neoclassical **Plaza de Toros,** one of the oldest bullrings in Spain. Inaugurated in 1785, it is regarded as the birthplace of the modern bullfight, and is something of a shrine to aficionados of the *corrida*. It has a small, but very interesting, museum below the arcaded arena.

Cádiz

The ancient city of **Cádiz,** sitting at the end of a very narrow peninsula of land that runs parallel to the coast, was founded by the Phoenicians in 1100 B.C. and is considered to be Spain's oldest town. In fact, Cádiz's amazing amalgam of history is not readily apparent, with only the remains of the old Roman Theater to give much evidence of the city's age. It was re-conquered by Alfonso X in 1262 and granted the Monopoly of Trade with Africa by the Catholic Monarchs in 1493. Columbus also departed from this city on his second and fourth voyages in 1493 and 1502, respectively. In the latter part of the 16th century, it twice came under attack by enemy naval forces, and a period of prosperity ensued when the Casa de Contratación, or the monopoly rights for trade with the Americas, was transferred from Sevilla by order of Felipe V in 1717. A century later on 19 March 1812, while under attack from Napoleon's forces, the national parliament met in the St. Felipe Neri Church and proclaimed the first Spanish parliament.

Of most interest in the town today is the architecturally contrasting Baroque and Classical **cathedral,** which was constructed between 1772 and 1838. The elegant **Hospital de Mujeres** (Women's Hospital), built even earlier in 1749, is notable for its patio and art collection, including a fine El Greco. The curious and unusual **Oratorio de la Santa Cueva** (Church of Santa Cueva) has original underground chapels dating from 1783. Of more interest is the domed upper chapel added in 1796, whose ceiling is adorned by five spectacular paintings—three of which are fine examples of Goya's work. The **St. Felipe Neri Church,** mentioned above, is also well worth a look. Built in 1679, it has towering columns and an unusual elliptical dome.

El Puerto de Santa María

This small town, on the coast of the Bay of Cádiz, looks across to the town of the same name and has considerable charm. It is generally overlooked by foreign visitors, but the

Carnival lights adorn the streets of the ancient city of Cádiz when it is time for a fiesta!

Spanish flock here in the thousands, especially during August. Then, when there are a series of bullfights, the seafood and shellfish restaurants for which El Puerto is famous are full to overflowing until the early hours. In fact, there isn't too much to see here, but that's okay—El Puerto de Santa María is one of those places that is to be savored for its ambience. Positioned between Jerez de la Frontera and Cádiz, El Puerto is easily reached by road or rail. However, the most delightful way to get here is on the small ferryboat, *El Adriano,* which plies its way between the center of Cádiz and the dockside in El Puerto.

Jerez de la Frontera

The name of this town is indicative of two things. It once lay close to the frontier of the old Moorish kingdom of Granada, hence *de la Frontera*. And *Jerez* (pronounced khay-*reth*) gave its name to the wine that has made the town famous, better known to the world in its anglicized version—sherry.

Although known as long ago as the Phoenician era, Jerez first came to prominence under the Moors in the 11th and 12th centuries, and it is from that period that the impressively walled and towered **Alcázar** dates. Inside is a simple but elegant mosque that was later converted into a chapel dedicated to Santa María la Real. Re-conquered by King Alfonso X in 1264, it became one of the most prosperous towns in Andalucía after the discovery of the Americas and the reunification of Spain in 1492.

Below the Alcázar lies the **Colegiata** (Collegiate Church), a towering dark stone cathedral dating from the 17th to 18th centuries. Housed within is the precious image of *Cristo de la Viña* (Christ of the Vineyard). It was the development of the sherry wine and brandy business that brought the city worldwide acclaim and more prosperity. It is impossible to walk the streets without recognizing *bodegas* (wineries) of prestigious old firms such as Harvey, Williams & Humbert, Gonzalez-Byass, and Pedro Domecq. As some of the names imply, it was a group of English merchants who launched Jerez as the world capital of fortified wine.

Three centuries on, their descendants continue to control the sherry trade. All the larger companies offer **tours** of their bodegas, mostly on weekday mornings, and some require you to reserve in advance. Traditional hospitality means of course that every tour ends with a tasting session.

> In Shakespeare's day, sherry wine was called sack or sherries sack. Sack is derived from the Spanish word *sacar* (to export) while sherries comes from the Anglicized name of the town where the first sherries were made, Jerez, or Sherry.

Jerez is also famous for its horses. The sherry-producing aristocracy built vast ranches alongside the vineyards, which provided an ideal environment for horse breeding. And the Domecq family established the world-famous Real Escuela Andaluza del Arte Ecuestre (Royal Andalucían Riding School) in 1973 as a showcase for Andalucían equestrian skills. The school's Thursday dressage exhibitions are a must-see, and the annual Horse Fair in early May is a colorful event.

Jerez has more subtle attractions also. In addition to the expected numerous churches, palaces, and mansions, look especially for the Andalucían Flamenco Center in the distinguished Pemartín Palace and the striking Clock Museum in its own delightful gardens.

Sevilla

The capital of Andalucía, Sevilla is the most Spanish of Spanish cities. One of the most beautiful cities in the world, it has a sensual, spiritual, and romantic ambience.

It was already a thriving riverside settlement when Julius Caesar arrived in 45 B.C., and under the Romans, it developed into a major town. In fact, two Roman emperors, Hadrian and Trajan, were born in nearby Itálica. Subsequently, Sevilla became the capital of the Visigothic kingdom and then of a Moorish taifa, before falling to King Ferdinand III in 1248. A monopoly of trade with the New World brought the city to its peak during the Golden Age. "Madrid is the capital of Spain," the saying went, "but Sevilla is the capital of the world."

Call ahead for a tour of a bodega—learn about wine-making and try some sherry.

The two most prominent monuments in the city are located around the Plaza del Triunfo. Work on the **cathedral,** the largest Gothic church in the world and the third largest of its kind—only St. Peter's in Rome and St. Paul's in London are bigger—began in 1401 after the great mosque was razed. The new building followed the ground plan of the old mosque, accounting for its unusually broad, rectangular form.

Massive without, and richly decorated within, the cathedral contains over 30 chapels, including the central **Capilla Mayor** with its Flemish altarpiece, and the **Capilla Real**

(Royal Chapel), last resting place of Ferdinand III, the "King-Saint" who delivered Sevilla from the hands of the infidel. The silver-gilt key to the city, presented to Ferdinand by the vanquished Moors, may be seen in the treasury, along with a cross made from the first gold brought back by Cristobal Colón (Christopher Columbus) from the New World. The Great Navigator himself is interred nearby, in the ornate 19th-century sarcophagus by the south entrance. His remains were transferred to Sevilla from Havana in 1898, when Cuba won its independence from Spain.

On the north side of the cathedral lies the **Patio de los Naranjos** (Court of the Orange Trees), the ceremonial courtyard of the old mosque with its original ablutions fountains. The minaret, dating from 1184, was preserved as the bell tower of the cathedral; this celebrated **Giralda** tower is Sevilla's most famous landmark. The exterior is beautifully decorated with typical *sebka* design work. It contrasts vividly with the bland interior, where a series of 35 gently elevating ramps lead to an observation platform at a height of 70 m (230 ft). Ferdinand III rode his horse to the top following the Reconquista in 1248.

This is the finest mirador in Sevilla, and provides for unparalleled views of the old city below. It is surprising to note just how large the Plaza de Toros is when seen at this angle. Look up and you will see how the tower came by its name. In 1356, an earthquake destroyed the original ornamental top. And it wasn't until 1558 that the addition of the huge bells and a weather vane (Giralda in Spanish) in the form of a statue of a beautiful goddess representing Faith, raised the height to 98 m (322 ft).

The Plaza del Triunfo sits at the heart of Sevilla—a great focal point for a day of sightseeing.

The Alcázar (entrance on far side of the square, through the Puerta del León) is a major monument to mid-14th century Mudéjar architecture, combining Moorish, Gothic, and Renaissance elements. Built by Moorish craftsmen under Christian rule, during the reign of Pedro the Cruel, the rambling palace and its several courtyards incorporate fragments of an earlier Moorish fortress, and blend Christian motifs with Moorish designs. A visit begins with a tour of the Cuarto del Almirante (the Admiral's Apartments), where a painting of the Virgen de los Mareantes (Virgin of the Mariners) in the chapel shows Columbus sheltered beneath the Virgin's cloak. The most interesting part is the Patio de las Doncellas (Courtyard of the Maidens), where the rooms preserve outstanding decorative features—ornamental tiles, carved stucco, and characteristic coffered *artesonado* ceilings.

The ornate, domed **Salón de Embajadores** (Hall of the Ambassadors) is equal to anything in the palace of the Alhambra. Next door is the glass-roofed Patio de las Muñecas (Courtyard of the Dolls), so named for the two tiny human faces carved into the decoration surrounding one of the Moorish arches. These are very unusual as Muslim craftsmen were forbidden by their religion to depict the human form in their art.

Returning to the entrance courtyard, take the narrow passage on the right to the Patio de Maria Padilla, which sits on top of underground baths. The apartments beyond are hung with Flemish tapestries recording Charles V's Tunis Expedition of 1535, one of them showing an upside-down map of the Mediterranean. Not to be missed, either, are the extensive and beautiful gardens, an oasis of tranquillity in this perpetually busy city.

Nestled around the walls of the Alcazar is the **Barrio de Santa Cruz,** the old Jewish quarter, a picturesque maze of whitewashed houses, narrow lanes, and tiny shaded patios that invite leisurely exploration. Just south of the cathedral stands the former exchange building, Casa Lonja, which is now the **Archivo de Indias.** The unusual Cuban wooden shelves are of interest as well as the documents relating to the discovery and conquest of the Americas that rest on them.

Nearby, on the banks of the river, is another of Sevilla's icons. The Moorish **Torre del Oro** (Tower of Gold) is named after the gold-colored tiles that once covered the walls of this early 13th-century chess-piece castle. It is all that remains of Sevilla's medieval fortifications, and in times of possible invasion a huge metal chain was hauled from here to the other riverbank to protect the harbor. Originally used to store treasures brought from

Mudéjar architecture incorporates all kinds of beautiful, unique details, as well as elements of traditional styles.

Go for the gold — check out the Torre del Oro, the last vestige of medieval Sevilla.

the Americas, it was also used as a prison and is now a maritime museum. The round top and spire were added in the middle of the 18th century. A visit to the **Museo de Bellas Artes** (Museum of Fine Arts), housed in an early 17th-century convent and the second most important museum in Spain, will remind visitors that Sevilla is the birthplace of two of Spain's greatest artists, Velázquez and Murillo.

There are, of course, far too many other places of interest to mention here, but those with a little extra time should visit the following. The **Casa de Pilatos,** the **Hospital de la Caridad** (Charity Hospital), the **Bullfighting Museum** and **Plaza de Toros,** the **Parque de los Descubrimientos** (Discovery Park) on the site of Expo '92, and the pedestrian shopping district centered on the **Calle de las Sierpes.** Don't forget that two of Europe's best-known festivals take place here each spring, the **Semana Santa** (Holy Week) parades and the *Fería de Abril* celebration.

Carmona

Carmona, 20 km or so (12 miles) east of Sevilla on the road to Córdoba, sits like a beacon on top of the only hill on an otherwise unrelenting plain. That position has given it strategic importance during its 5,000-year old history. It was the Roman era, though, that brought the area prosperity and wealth, and the **Museo y Necropolis** is the largest Roman necropolis outside of Rome itself.

The town's fortunes declined after the Romans left, but the Moorish invasion of 713 brought with it renewed growth and prosperity. The Moors' reign ended in 1247 when Carmona was re-conquered by King Ferdinand II. The town was divided among the victors, principally the orders of Santiago and Calatrava. The 14th and 15th centuries were troublesome times as well. The discord was only brought to an end when, in 1630, Felipe IV agreed to grant Carmona the rights of township.

Carmona's history is also unique because the town was never under feudal rule, and was protected as a satellite of the crown. It is for this reason that there is such an extraordinary number of palaces, mansions, convents, and churches in Carmona. These alone make it worth a visit, and the two gates that linked the old *card maxim* (Roman road), **Displays** (Sevilla) and **Cordoba** (Córdoba), shouldn't be missed. (Displays is especially interesting; the gate is an unusually shaped small fortress.)

Córdoba

These days, Córdoba, a minor provincial city sandwiched between Sevilla and Granada, is often passed over by visitors to Andalucía. But to do so is a considerable mistake. Besides having much charm, it has fabulous historic connections and an eclectic array of attractions to match. Córdoba was once the largest city in Roman Spain, the capital of the province of Batik, and the birthplace of Seneca the Younger, philosopher and tragedian.

Its golden era was between the mid-8th and very early 11th centuries when it was the center of the great medieval Caliphate of Córdoba. With a population of half a million, it was one of the world's largest and most cultured cities and the splendid capital of the western Islamic Empire. It had the first university and street lighting in Europe, and a library with more than 400,000 volumes.

The city is dominated by the greatest surviving monument from that period (which has the distinction of being the oldest monument in day-to-day use in the Western world)—the Great Mosque, otherwise known as **La Mezquita**. Construction on the mosque was begun in 786, but it was enlarged three times before attaining its present size in 987. It covers an astounding area of 2 hectares (5 acres). Córdoba was reconquered in 1236, and two small Christian chapels were added in 1258 and 1260. No further major changes were made until the early 16th century when Carlos V decided to construct a Christian cathedral in the center of the mosque.

Several gateways provide access through the high wall surrounding La Mezquita, the most impressive being the monumental Mudéjar **Puerta del Perdón** (Gate of Forgiveness). Pass through it into the ceremonial forecourt of the **Patio de los Naranjos**, with its fountains and venerable orange trees, to reach the entrance to the mosque. Inside, as your eyes adjust to the dim light, you will see mesmerizing rows of columns extending into the shadows in every direction. Antique shafts of porphyry, onyx, marble, and jasper, they seem to grow out of the paving stones like trees in an enchanted forest. The double arches overhead, striped in red-and-white, form a fanciful canopy of curving branches.

At the far end, set in the southeast wall, is the splendid 10th-century **mihrab**, lined with marble and gold mosaics, and the **maksourah**, the enclosure where the caliph attended to his prayers. In the central area of the mosque, restorers have exposed to view a section of the original carved and painted wooden ceiling, which was covered over with vaulting in the 18th century.

The **cathedral**, found at the very center of the forest of pillars, presents an over-powering contrast to its immediate surroundings. The understated simplicity—and lack of human images—of Islamic design fades completely and is replaced with an ornate blaze of color within which human images in either paint, stone, or wood abound. Around the walls more Christian chapels line the perimeter of the mosque.

Aptly built during Córdoba's "golden era," La Mezquita has a most ornate interior.

North of the La Mezquita lies the labyrinth of narrow streets that makes up the **Barrio de la Judería** (Jewish Quarter). Some of the best restaurants and *tapas* bars in Córdoba are to be found here. Sights to look for include the Callejon de las Flores (Alley of the Flowers), which is lined with houses built around flower-filled patios that are typical of Córdoba, and the 14th-century *sinagoga* (**synagogue**) in the street called Judios. It's a modest affair, just one small room, with a balcony for female worshippers. Córdoba's Jews helped the Moors to gain control of the city in 711, and they lived in peace under the caliphate.

Perhaps the most illustrious resident of the neighborhood was Moses Maimónides. And a statue of the 12th-century doctor, philosopher, and theologian stands a few steps from the synagogue in the square named in his honor, **Plaza de Maimónides**. Also in the plaza is the **Casa de las Bulas**, which holds the interesting combination of a small market of Córdoban craftspeople selling silver filigree and tooled leather goods, and the **Museo Taurino** (Bullfighting Museum).

Northeast of the mosque on the Plaza Jerónimo Paéz, the splendid Renaissance Palacio Paéz houses the **Museo Arqueológico Provincial**. The exhibits span the centuries from the Iberian era to the Visigothic period, but pride of place goes to objects from the 10th-century palace of Medina Azahara, like the bronze figure of a stag taken from a fountain presented by the Byzantine emperor Constantine VII.

A Christian king, Alfonso XI, built Córdoba's **Alcázar de los Reyes Cristianos**, overlooking the river to the southwest of the mosque. The ramparts offer a fine view over the old town and the river, the islets in midstream each occupied by a ruined Moorish mill, and the ridges of the Sierra de Córdoba low on the northern horizon. The Catholic Monarchs received Columbus and planned the invasion of Granada while residents here.

Other places that are worth a visit are the 16th century **Palacio de los Marqueses de Viana**, with its 13 patios, and the **Plaza de la Corredera**, dating from the 17th century. It is the only Castilian-style plaza in Andalucía. Stroll to the unusual **Plaza del Potro**, which gets its name from the fountain in the center dating from 1577. It is home to two interesting museums: the **Museo de Bellas Artes** (Fine Arts Museum) and the ever-popular **Julio Romero de Torres Museum**, a museum devoted to the Córdoban artist of the same name. He was born nearby and specialized in mildly erotic paintings of rather beautiful Córdobése women.

Eight kilometers (5 miles) west of Córdoba lies the ruins of the intriguing city cum palace of **Medina Azahara**. It was commissioned in 936 by Abdel-Rahman III in honor of his favorite concubine Al Zahra (The Flower), and its design was so grand that detailed records indicate that building materials were brought from Constantinople and other North African locations. Despite such auspicious beginnings, it had a short life; the palace was razed with the breakup of the Caliphate of Córdoba in the very early 11th century. Many of the materials were subsequently used on constructions in Sevilla and other towns. For nearly 900 years, it was left in ruins, and not until 1910 did the slow work of excavation begin. This still continues, but reconstructed royal apartments give some impression of the original magnificence of this sumptuous complex of baths, schools, gardens, and

Off to the summer place for the weekend — Medina Azahara was once a modest royal getaway.

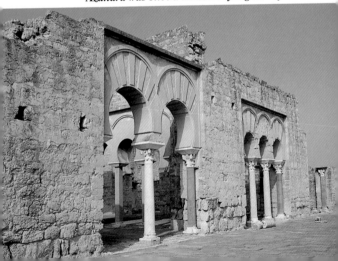

There is no shortage of breathtaking views throughout the Costa del Sol.

stately apartments built on three terraces.

Alcalá la Real

The road from Córdoba to Granada is, in many sections, rather dramatic; you pass through mountainous scenery dotted with small white-walled towns often crowned with castles. **Alcalá la Real**, as it was known in Roman times, was a Moorish fortified city from the early 8th century and remained a strategic bastion until the re-conquest of Granada in 1492, after which further Christian monuments were added. The **Fortaleza de la Mota**, on the summit at 1,033 m (3,389 ft), is a very amazing complex combining Moorish and Christian influences, along with spectacular views. A particular fascination, and one both beautiful and gruesome, is the semi-ruined church whose floor has been partly excavated leaving tombs with bones and skulls exposed.

Granada

The Nasrid dynasty rose to power in Granada just as the fortunes of the Spanish Moors were beginning to wane (see page 15). The first of the line, Mohammed ben Alhamar, established his capital here in 1232, after Ferdinand III had forced him from Jaén. Two years later, Moors fleeing from the newly vanquished Sevilla swelled the population, which had already been augmented by refugees from Córdoba. Rather than grieve for the homes they had left behind, the industrious Moors set about making Granada the grandest city of Al Andalus. Over the course of the next century, the hilltop palace of the Alhambra took shape. Granada was the last of the great Moorish kingdoms of Andalucía to be re-conquered, and King Boabdil's surrender to the Catholic Monarchs in January 1492 marked the end of the Muslim Empire in Spain.

The second most visited monument in Spain is the world-famous **Alhambra** (The Red). It takes its name from the red-brown bricks used in the construction of its outer walls, which rise precipitously above the deep gorge of the Río Darro. Its towers, strategically, command superb views over the city below.

Within the walls of the Alhambra, there are four main areas to explore, which are best taken in the following order: the **Alcazaba** (fortress), the **Casa Real Vieja** (Old Royal Palace), the **Casa Real Nueva** (new Royal Palace), and final-ly the **Generalife** (summer gardens). Amazingly, this com-plex was allowed to fall into almost total disrepair over the centuries, and was used as a barracks for Napoleon's troops during the Wars of Independence. It wasn't until 1870 that it was designated a National Monument.

The Alcazaba is the oldest part of the Alhambra and only the impressive outer walls and towers survive. The main attraction is the view from the Torre de la Vela, north over Albaicín and Sacromonte and south to the high snow-capped peaks of the Sierra Nevada.

The Palacio Nazares is the highlight of the monument. It was the magnificent home of the rulers of the kingdom of Granada. Actually a series of palaces, not just one, each palace

*Clearly a popular sight for tourists, the Palacio Nazares is
an attraction of monumental intrigue.*

home has its own patios, fountains, pools, and other adorn-
ments. The intricacy, delicacy, and bountiful beauty of the
design creates a visual impression that is beyond mere words.

The **Salón de Embajadores** (Hall of the Ambassadors),
or royal audience chamber, is one of the most sumptuously
ornamented rooms in the Alhambra. Skirted with geometric
tiling, the walls and roof are overlaid with delicately shaped
plaster stalactites, reaching 18 m (60 ft) to the carved and
painted wooden ceiling. Verses from the Koran and the name
of the 14th-century monarch Yusuf I are woven into the
design. Through the tall, arched windows are magnificent
views of Albaicín and the Darro. The **Sala de Abencerrajes**
recalls the aristocratic family of that name, who was accused
of disloyalty and collusion with the Christians by Boabdil.
The king invited the Abencerrajes to a reception in this very

room, and massacred all 36 of the unsuspecting family members. The **Patio de los Leones**, whose name derives from the splashing fountain in the center upheld by 12 stone lions, the **Torre de las Damas** (Tower of the Ladies), and the old bath area are of particular interest also.

The Casa Real Nueva, though imposing, is as the name implies relatively new and architecturally at odds with the more ornate older palaces, some of which were destroyed to make way for it. Commissioned by Carlos V in 1527, its exterior is in the shape of a square, with a surprisingly elegant two-story circular patio on the inside. Considered on its own merits, the building must be regarded as a fine example of Renaissance architecture.

Two museums are housed inside the palace. The first, the **Museo Nacional de Arte Hispano-Musulmán** (Museum of Hispano-Moorish Art), displays such evocative artifacts as the throne of the Nasrids, a wooden armchair inlaid with silver and ivory, and the Alhambra Vase, which once graced the Hall of the Two Sisters. The second, known as the **Museo de Bellas Artes** (Fine Arts Museum), contains a collection of works chronicling the development of the school of Granada between the 16th and 19th centuries.

The Generalife is found at the eastern end of the Alhambra fortifications on the neighboring hillside. A modest summer palace, it is surrounded by beautiful terraced gardens where oleander and roses bloom luxuriantly and delicate fountains and cascades play among the neatly clipped cypress hedges.

Back down in the city, the most prominent monument is the exquisite **Capilla Real** (Royal Chapel), a Renaissance chapel that serves as the mausoleum of the Catholic Monarchs. The effigies of Ferdinand and Isabella lie on the right-hand side of the chancel, with those of their daughter Juana La Loca and her husband Felipe El Hermoso on the slightly higher monument on the left. Their mortal remains have been interred in the crypt underneath since 1521, after a ceremonial transfer of their remains from the Alhambra. On exhibition in the **sacristy** are mementos of the Catholic Monarchs, including Ferdinand's sword and Isabella's scepter and crown, a circle of gold embellished with acanthus scrolls.

The cathedral next door is large and imposing. A few steps away is the **Alcaicería** area, the old silk market of the Moors. These days, it is a colorful collection of narrow lanes that serve as a center for the sale of handicrafts and souvenirs. Not far away is the **Corral del Carbón** (House of Coal). Dating from the 12th century, it is the oldest Moorish monument in the city, and is now a center for typical Granadino arts and crafts.

Albaicín, the old Moorish district on the hill opposite the Alhambra, has a maze of narrow streets and staircases surrounding its ancient whitewashed houses and enclosed patio gardens. Down by the Darro River is the exquisite **Casa de**

The Catholic Monarchs are memorialized atop their burial crypt inside the Capilla Real.

Castril, dating from 1539 and home of the Archaeological Museum as well as nearby 11th-century **El Bañuelo** (Moorish baths). Farther up the hill is the **Mirador San Nicolás**. From here, you get the best view of the Alhambra framed by the snowcapped Sierra Nevada mountains in the background—a scene replicated on many postcards. High to the right of Albaicín is the **Gitano** (Gypsy) area of Sacramonte, famous for its caves and **tablaos** (literally stages) where gypsies, for the benefit of tourists, reenact wedding ceremonies. Tourists, though, should be wary, especially at night, as this is not the safest part of town.

Lying about 50 km (32 miles) east of Granada on the road to Murcia is **Guadix**, a particularly unusual city in that many of its inhabitants are troglodytes. In the Barrio Santiago, there are streets with houses that have their own small front yards and façades that, on the surface, make them indistinguishable from ordinary homes. Look closely, though, and the white, circular chimneys emanating from the rocks give the game away. These are actually caves with a practical use: they're cool in summer and warm in winter. There is plenty else of interest here, including a Moorish castle dating from the 10th and 11th centuries, a late 16th-century cathedral, and many important palaces, houses, and churches.

Washington Irving

Irving was an American writer who is best known for *The Sketch Book*, a collection of stories that included such classics as *The Legend of Sleepy Hollow* and *Rip Van Winkle*. From 1826 until 1832, he was attached to the American legation in Spain, where he became fascinated by the legends of Moorish Andalucía. During his stay in Granada, he moved into the apartments of Charles V while writing *Tales of the Alhambra*, a collection of stories about Granada's Moorish past.

Las Alpujarras

Shop for souvenirs and handicrafts in the narrow lanes of Grenada's Alcaicería.

This is a remote area even today, located as it is between the Sierra Nevada and Sierra de la Contraviesa mountain ranges, with the southern slopes of the latter dropping graciously into the Mediterranean Sea. Not particularly pretty, it is dotted with small towns and villages that retain many appearances of a lifestyle long since departed from other areas. The way of life here in the early 20th century was detailed explicitly by Gerald Brenan in his book *South from Granada*. In fact, these communities fall into one of two areas depending on their altitude and climate; those in **La Alpujarra Alta** (the high Alpujarra), just south of the highest peaks in the Sierra Nevada and those in **La Alpujarra Baja** (the low Alpujarra) in the Sierra de la Contraviesa. Trevelez, considered the highest village in Spain, is famous for its *jamón serrano* (dried cured ham), and Lanjarón is familiar throughout Spain as the name on the red, green, and white label on bottles of water originating from the town's springs. Incidentally, that same water runs free from the *fuentes* (fountains) of many villages.

The main entrance to Las Alpujarras is from the Granada to Motril road; the same road along which the defeated Moors traveled on their way to exile. Even today, there is a place on that road, just 12 km (8 miles) south of Granada, that bears the sad name **El Puerto del Suspiro del Moro** (the Pass of the Sigh of the Moor). It is from here that distant Granada finally fades from view, and the land takes its name from the comments made by the defeated King Boabdil's mother when he, supposedly, wept while looking back at the city. Somewhat cruelly, she is reported to have told him, "Don't cry like a woman for something you couldn't defend as a man."

Andalucía's Natural Parks

Andalucía has an abundance of natural parks, ranging from those with international fame to more obscure, remote nature preserves. Below some of the most interesting are described.

The Sierra Morena This nearly 480 km (300-mile) mountain range runs from the mountains of southern Portugal in the west to the border of the Provincia de Murcia in the east, effectively forming the border between Andalucía and most of the rest of Spain.

Covering an area of 524,000 hectares (1,290,000 acres), the Sierra Morena encompasses no fewer than seven natural parks, namely: the Sierra de Aracena y Picos de Aroche; the Sierra Norte de Sevilla; the Sierra de Hornachuelos; the Sierra Cardeña y Montoro; the Sierra de Andújar; Despeñaperros; and the Sierra de Cazorla, Segurla y Las Villas.

Each of these parks has its own attributes, and the whole area is a stronghold of the Spanish Lynx, but the highest peaks and the most dramatic scenery is found in the last of these, which is also the birthplace of the great Guadalquivir River.

Doñana National Park This is probably the most famous park in Spain. It holds many national and international honors, and is even listed as a World Heritage Site. Consisting of 86,208 hectares (213,020 acres), it is bordered on two sides by the Atlantic Ocean and the Guadalquivir River as it winds its way down from Sevilla to reach the ocean at Sanlúcar de

Barrameda. In fact, Doñana is the last great lowland wilderness sanctuary in southern Europe, and has three distinct ecosystems: the *marismas* (salt marshes), *matorral* (brushwood), and *las dunas* (sand dunes). Within its bounds can be found an amazing array of animal, bird, and plant life, but what you see is very much dependent upon the time of year you visit and, even then, can be very hit or miss.

The only way to really see the park is on a tour organized by Coop. Andaluz Marismas del Rocío, whose large-wheel buses depart from the visitors' center at El Acebuche. Be forewarned, though: this is a very bumpy, rough ride, and definitely not advisable for those with artificial hips or physical handicaps. Lasting about four hours, it enters the sand dunes at Matalascañas and the first part of the trip is along 35 km (nearly 20 miles) of unspoiled beaches. The only human residents here are the fishermen living in what look like very ramshackle huts, albeit with 4-wheel drive vehicles and TV antennas on display. The vast stretches of salt marshes are fascinating, with many animals living along the edge of the grassland adjoining them. The huge sand dunes, perpetually changing, make for a surreal sight.

Laguna de Medina Across the Guadalquivir and just about 10 km (6 miles) east of Jerez de la Frontera is this small lake, one of the last stops in Europe for birds migrating south from northern and central Europe to Africa at the end of August. In periods of drought it is attractive to birds that usually reside at Doñana, and around 50 species have been observed here.

Grazalema A short distance to the east of Laguna de Medina is the mainly mountain wilderness of the natural park of Grazalema. Its 51,695 hectares (127,740 acres) are home to three species of eagles and numerous other birds, mammals, and reptiles. Interestingly, the mountains here, which range between 1,000 and 1,700 meters (3,300 and 5,600 ft), are the first stop for clouds arriving from the Atlantic, giving the area the greatest annual rainfall in Spain. This allows a fine array of flora to thrive. Of particular note is the rare *abies pinsapo* (Spanish fir tree).

El Torcal de Antequera and the Fuente de Piedra Just south of the city of Antequera is one of the more famous geological formations in Spain. The limestone mountains of the El Torcal de Antequera have eroded to form some of the most unusual shapes seen anywhere. In fact, these formations so resemble modern sculptures that they have been assigned comical names. Just north of Antequera, droughts notwithstanding, is the Fuente de Piedra, Andalucía's largest lake, with a surface area that can reach 1,384 hectares (3,420 acres). Each spring, provided that weather conditions are favorable, it becomes a home to flamingos. In fact, it is the only inland breeding area in Europe for this colorful species. Springtime means the islet of La Colonia becomes one of the most crowded bird habitats anywhere (more than 16,000 breeding pairs were identified in 1996). Over 150 species of birds have been counted on the lake or in surrounding areas.

Sierra Nevada & Las Alpujarras This recently created national park, which begins near Granada, has the distinction of having the highest peak on the Spanish mainland (Mulhacén is 3,482 meters (11,420 ft) tall) and a wide diversity of flora made possible by the nearby Mediterranean Biosphere Reserve. It also has the highest road in Europe. Along it is the Solynieve (literally Sun and Snow) skiing resort, accessible year-round at some 2,500 m (8,000 ft), and the more elevated Pico Veleta (the Weathercock) at 3,398 m (11,148 ft), which can only be reached during a few short weeks in summer.

WHAT TO DO

SPORTS

Most visitors to the Costa del Sol do not plan daytime activities more energetic than lazing on the beach, and save their energy for nightlife. However, sports facilities are in abundance for those who want to work off the effects of too much paella during the daylight hours.

Water Sports

The main resort beaches offer all kinds of sports equipment for rent, as well as beach umbrellas and loungers. The larger beach restaurants have toilet facilities, and some provide changing rooms.

Swimming: With more than 160 km (100 miles) of beaches, the Costa del Sol offers plenty of spots for swimming. Most of the sandy strands lie to the west of Málaga, while shingle and rocks (with some sandy coves) predominate to the east. In the high season, the most popular beaches are mobbed. You stand the best chance of finding a patch of sand to yourself to the east of Nerja and west of Estepona.

Many beaches now fly the blue EU flag, which means that water quality and general sanitation meets environmental standards established by the European Union.

Boating: There are numerous marinas along the coast between Málaga and Sotogrande, providing year-round moorings for yachts and motor boats. Some offer boats for day rentals and longer-term charters (with or without captain and crew). Marbella boasts three such establishments, and many of the beaches and larger beach hotels rent sailboats.

Waterskiing: The main resorts all have water skiing schools, and most big hotels offer instruction. Prices are generally high, but they do vary. Swimming and skiing areas often overlap.

Windsurfing: This sport is the coast's fastest-growing activity, with boards, sails, and professional instruction available in most of the resort areas. The season runs from March to November with strongest winds in June and September.

Snorkeling and Scuba Diving: Snorkeling can be an engrossing activity, particularly off the rocky, indented stretch of coast beyond Nerja. If you dive or snorkel any distance from the shore, you are legally required to tow a marker buoy. Diving centers operate in several resorts. For more information, contact the local tourist office (see page 124).

Angling: Fishing from the rocks and breakwaters is a popular pastime with the locals and a permit is not required. The deeper waters offshore teem with tunny (tuna), swordfish, and shark. Deep-sea fishing boats can be rented at the marinas, and many resort hotels make arrangements for fishing expeditions.

A very popular inland fishing spot is the Pantanos del Chorro (*pantano* meaning "reservoir") at the Chorro Dam (see page 29). Freshwater anglers must have a permit — ask at the nearest tourist office for information on how to obtain one.

Other Sports

Golf: When it comes to variety, few resort areas in the world can compare with the

Many of the world's finest golfers have enjoyed the greens near Marbella.

Costa del Sol. There are nearly 30 18-hole courses between Málaga and Gibraltar. Most private and hotel clubs welcome non-residents or non-members, though some may charge visitors a higher fee. Clubs, caddies, and carts are generally available for rental.

The quality of the courses is excellent — many have been designed by such famous names as Robert Trent Jones and Seve Ballesteros. Las Brisas, near Marbella, has hosted the Spanish Open and Valderrama, near Sotogrande, was host to the 1997 Ryder Cup. Although a private club, Valderrama has nine starting times between midday and 2pm that are open to the public, albeit at 30,000 ptas (€180.3) per round.

For details of golf courses and fees, consult the monthly magazine *Costa Golf*, an English-language publication.

Tennis and Squash: Some of the biggest names in tennis are linked to the numerous clubs, centers, and "ranches" on the Costa del Sol, including the Marbella-based Manolo Santana Tennis Club, which hosts the majority of Spain's Davis Cup matches and other important tournaments.

Bicycling: Bikes can be rented at towns up and down the coast and inland (where mountain roads and trails are ideal for mountain biking).

Hiking: There are a number of good hiking areas within easy reach of the coast, notably the Montes de Málaga National Park just north of Málaga and El Torcal and El Chorro a little farther inland (see page 28). For more good walks, try the area around Ronda, and the hills above the Refugio de Juanar near Marbella (see page 41).

Hunting: The foothills of the Sierra Nevada harbor rabbit and partridge, while deeper in the mountains lurk deer. There are hunting grounds in the area north of Marbella, especially in the Serranía de Ronda and, closer to the coast, the Sierra Blanca (see page 41). The season for game runs roughly from the months of September–December, while small animals may generally be hunted from October– February. A hunting permit is required.

Horseback Riding: Andalucía is famous for both its horses and horsemanship. There are stables on the coast and near the inland cities, with mounts for rent; you can canter along the open beach or ride up into the hills.

Skiing: Few people think of the Costa del Sol as a ski resort, but skiing can be enjoyed between December and May at the Solynieve resort near Granada, 160 km (100 miles) northeast of Málaga in the Sierra Nevada. Situated near the summit of mount Veleta, it is Europe's southernmost ski resort.

SHOPPING

Most establishments are open from 9:30 or 10am–1:30 or 2:00pm and from 4:30–8:00pm. The siesta (see below) is still religiously observed in southern Spain. In summer, shops in the tourist resorts keep longer hours, staying open all day until 8:30pm or sometimes later. Department stores do not close for the siesta.

The Spanish government levies a value-added tax (called IVA) on most items (currently up to 13.8%). Tourists from outside the EU will be refunded the IVA they pay on purchases above a minimum of 15,000 ptas (€90.15) or US$100 in stores where they see the TAX FREE SHOPPING logo. Whenever

> ### Siesta
>
> The *siesta* is an afternoon nap taken to avoid the hottest part of the day. What it means for the visitor is that many shops and businesses take a three-hour lunch break, closing from 1 or 2pm–4 or 5pm, and then opening up again until 7:30pm. This age-old custom seems to be dying out in some parts of northern Spain, but it is still observed in Andalucía.

you make a purchase, simply ask for a Global Refund Check. Then when you declare your purchases at Customs, your check will be validated. The check can then be cashed at a nearby Cash Refund Office or at any of the International Cash Refund offices worldwide. Another option that may be more convenient is to mail the check to a Cash Refund Office and have your credit card account automatically credited. It's worthwhile if you plan on spending a lot in one place.

> **When does the…open/shut?**
> *¿A qué hora abre/cierra…?*

Markets

Weekly open-air markets are held Mondays in Marbella, Tuesdays in Nerja and Fuengirola, Wednesdays in Estepona, Thursdays in Torremolinos and San Pedro de Alcántara, and Fridays in Benalmádena. Most cities have a *rastro* (flea market) on Sunday morning. Of these, Sevilla's is the largest and the town also has a coin-and-stamp and small animal market on the same day.

Where to Shop

The larger cities offer lower prices and a better selection of goods than resorts like Torremolinos or Fuengirola. The El Corte Inglés department store in Málaga, Sevilla, and other places is also well worth looking for.

For more sophisticated shopping, nothing can compare with Marbella or Puerto Banús, where dozens of attractive harbor-front boutiques offer a stunning selection of merchandise at equally stunning prices.

You can make a considerable saving on luxury goods like jewelry, watches, perfumes, and Havana cigars in duty-free Gibraltar, where the dreaded VAT does not exist.

Ceuta, the Spanish protectorate on the North African coast, has special tax status and alcohol, for example, is vastly cheaper there than mainland Spain. The same applies to electrical goods etc., but these will not seem like much of a bargain for Americans.

What to Buy

Traditional Spanish handicrafts are high on any souvenir-hunter's shopping list.

Ceramics: Everyday glazed terracotta pottery can be bought all along the coast. There's also a wide selection of tiles (*azulejos*), vases, bowls, and jugs, with floral or geometric decorations in bright colors.

Foodstuffs: Take home a taste of Spain with some olives, olive oil, almonds, cheese, or mouthwatering candies and cookies.

Jewelry: Silver rings, bracelets, and necklaces in modern designs make good buys, as do the artificial Majorica pearls of Spain. Look, too, for fine filigree jewelry from Córdoba, and smooth, polished olive wood beads.

Leather and Suede: Choose from a wide selection of handbags, belts, wallets, trousers, skirts, and coats. Leather goods, while no longer the bargain they once were, compare favorably in price with Italian and French made articles, and the local factories do turn out stylish, high-quality leather clothing. Córdoba, which has been producing leather goods since Roman times, is famous for its embossed leather.

Be sure to wrap souvenir plates carefully — you may want to carry them home.

Beware, though, many of the leather goods you will see have been imported from Morocco and are sold at vastly inflated prices. It's actually cheaper, and much more interesting, to take a day trip to Tangier and buy such goods there.

Souvenirs: Often delightfully tacky, from plastic castanets and flamenco dolls to imitation wineskins and even bullfight posters printed with your own name.

Wine and Spirits: Sweet Málaga wine, sherry, brandy, and Spanish wines provide some of the best bargains in Spain, and are generally cheaper when bought in a supermarket than at the last minute at the duty-free shop in the airport.

ENTERTAINMENT

Tour operators offer any number of excursions, some more esoteric than others, with brochures and booking facilities available through your hotel or a local travel agent. Another form of organized entertainment, amusement parks, are discussed below in the section for families with young children.

Bullfights: Andalucía is famed for its bullfighting traditions, and has two, Sevilla and Córdoba, of the seven first-class *Plaza de Toros* (bullrings) in Spain. The provincial capitals of Almería, Granada, Huelva, Jaén, and Málaga as well as Algeciras and El Puerto de Santa María are second-class rings. All others, including those of the resort towns along the Costa del Sol, come into the third class category. The two main events are a *Corrida de Toros*, where fully qualified matadors fight fully-grown — at least 4 year old — *toros* (bulls), and *Novilladas*, where *novilleros* (novice matadors) fight *novillos* (immature bulls).

As a rule of thumb, the better events are held in the better plazas, particularly during the *ferías* (holiday fairs) held in the major cities. Equally true is the fact that most of the events held in the resort towns are mainly for the benefit of tourists,

Some resorts have lavish productions that take the dramatic tradition of flamenco to the performance stage.

and are of lesser quality. They are not generally less expensive, though; small rings mean fewer seats, which often equates to higher prices. Contrary to popular opinion, bullfights are not held every Sunday in each city. In fact, outside of the ferías — when they are held daily — only Sevilla has them on a regular basis throughout the season. In other places, with the exception of Easter Sunday and August 15 — important national holidays — they are held sporadically and advertised by way of the ubiquitous *carteles* (posters) stuck on every wall. Be warned, though, these events are never less than bloody — and can be much worse. They are, however, enthralling spectacles, and whatever your reaction, you'll gain a valuable insight into the country and the people.

Flamenco: All the coastal resorts offer flamenco shows for tourists. These shows can be entertaining, but the performances are more show business than the true spirit of flamenco. To experience flamenco at its most authentic, you will have to search out bars and small clubs in Málaga or Sevilla. Ask the local tourist office for advice on where to go.

Flamenco is an ancient art form, combining elements of Visigothic, Moorish, and gypsy music. There are two distinct types; the *cante jondo* (deep song), an intense outpouring of emotion, and the animated *cante chico* (light song). There are also different varieties of flamenco dance (the *tango*, *fandango*, *farruca*, and *zambra*) performed to the staccato rhythms and counter-rhythms of the castanets, hand clapping (*palmadas*), and finger snapping (*pitos*), as well as furious heel-drumming (*zapateado*). There is no need to speak Spanish to enjoy the spectacle — you simply have to feel the music.

Discotheques and Nightclubs: Some discos open as early as 9pm, but most don't gear up for business until 11pm or midnight. They close late, too, around 4am or even later. Nightclubs (*salas de fiesta*) usually stage two shows an evening, one at about midnight or 1am and the other around 3am. Depending on the club, the show may feature flamenco performances, drag acts, or shows with semi-nude women. Bars, pubs, and clubs often provide musical entertainment.

Casinos: Two gambling establishments operate from 8pm to the early hours; the Casino Torrequebrada in Benalmádena-Costa, and the Casino Marbella, under the Hotel Andalucía Plaza in Puerto Banús. In addition to the usual games, the casinos have a bar, restaurant, and nightclub on the premises. Formal dress (jacket and tie for gentlemen) is required. Don't forget to bring your passport along for identification.

Concerts: From May to October, Tívoli World brings the stars of rock and pop to Torremolinos for concerts in the open air. The season's program may include performances of flamenco and *zarzuela* (Spanish light opera). In winter, Málaga's symphony orchestra performs in the Teatro Cervantes theater, and guest artists appear at Castillo El Bil-Bil in Benalmádena-Costa.

CHILDREN ON THE COSTA DEL SOL

The Costa del Sol is an ideal place for vacationing families with kids — it is, after all, one long beach. Apart from paddling and sandcastles, older children can learn how to sail, waterski, or windsurf. If you don't feel happy about letting your children play in the sea, especially the younger ones, the water parks at Mijas, Torremolinos, and Estepona offer a safer and more controlled environment where it's easier to keep a close eye on them.

Alternative diversions for children include the aquariums in Benalmádena and Puerto Banús, the Eagle Park in Benalmádena, the Cueva (cave) De Nerja, and Mini-Hollywood near Almería. In the evenings, Tívoli World near Benalmádena provides all the fun of the fair, with carnival rides and a roller coaster, and there's also a bar and flamenco show for the grownups. The Crocodile Park just north of Málaga will intrigue most children, as will the horse shows of El Ranchito in Benalmádena and Aires del Sur in Estepona.

When you're on the beach, don't forget that kids are especially vulnerable to the effects of too much sun. Take along plenty of high-factor sunscreen and sun hats, and make sure they're covered up during the middle of the day (a siesta during the hottest part of the day may be a good idea to avoid sunburn).

High speed thrills await the kids at Tívoli World, named for Denmark's famous park.

Calendar of Events

January: *Cabalgata de Reyes* (Three Kings Parade), Málaga. On the eve of Epiphany (5 January), floats, bands, and traditionally costumed characters commemorate the visit of the Wise Men to the infant Christ.

March/April: *Semana Santa* (Holy Week), throughout the area. Somber processions of hooded penitents and religious images take place nightly during the week before Easter. Most impressive in Sevilla, where accommodation is impossible to obtain. Málaga and Granada are other choices.

April: *Feria de Abril* (April Fair), Sevilla. Horses and riders, bullfights, flamenco, fireworks, and parties in the streets are part of Andalucía's most colorful festival.

April/May: *Feria del Caballo* (Horse Fair), Jerez de la Frontera. Spain's equestrian showcase, with events of all kinds, including racing, dressage, and carriage competitions.

May: *Romería de San Isidro* (Pilgrimage of St. Isidore), Estepona, Nerja. Decorated carts and costumed riders parade in Estepona, while Nerja stages concerts, folk dancing, and fireworks.

June: *Corpus Christi,* throughout the area. Bullfights and fireworks enliven this national holiday, a big event in Granada.

June/July: *Festival Internacional de Música y Danza,* Granada. Concerts and dance performed outdoors in the Alhambra and Generalife.

July: *Virgen del Carmen,* coastal towns. Processions of fishing boats pay tribute to the Virgin of Carmen, protector of fishermen.

August: *Feria de Málaga* (Málaga Fair), Málaga. A carnival, circus, bullfights, and flamenco events enliven the first fortnight of the month. *Festival de España,* Nerja. The town's famous cave provides the eerie venue for this subterranean celebration of music and dance.

September: *Feria de Ronda* (Ronda Fair), Ronda. The highlight of this fair is the *corrida goyesca,* a costumed bullfight held in Ronda's 18th-century ring. *Fiesta de la Vendímia* (Wine Harvest Festival), Jerez de la Frontera. A parade, bullfights, flamenco, and horse events follow the blessing of the harvest.

EATING OUT

You could easily spend your entire holiday on the Costa del Sol without ever sitting down to a Spanish meal. In the big coastal resorts the range of eating places is amazing: hamburger stands, pizza bars, pub grub, beach barbecues, and restaurants of almost any nationality you can think of, with a few Spanish ones thrown in for good measure. In fact, you could dine on bacon and eggs, beans on toast, steak and fries, and any other British staple every day, without going into the same restaurant twice. For those visitors adventurous enough to want to sample the local cuisine, however, there are numerous fine Spanish restaurants on the coast, and many, many more throughout Andalucía.

WHERE TO EAT

One of Spain's most civilized institutions is the **tapas** bar, or *tasca*. Originally, the idea was that when you ordered a drink, generally beer or wine only, a small helping of a tasty morsel and a couple of pieces of bread were given free. The food was served on a small plate traditionally used to cover the glass, and came to be called a *tapa*, which literally means "lid." These days such bars, especially in the resorts, are hard to find. More often than not there's a charge, usually from 100 ptas (€0.60) to 250 ptas (€1.50), depending upon what you choose. Although this is still a charming habit, and a fine way of sampling many different dishes, it can very quickly become costlier than selecting an inexpensive *menú del día* (set menu).

A *comedor,* or dining room, is often a small area at the back of a bar where you can sit down and dig into a basic but satisfying meal. Comedors tend, on the whole, to cater to local workers: cheap and cheerful, they are usually open for lunch only.

Beachfront cafés are festive places to get a quick bite to eat or wile away the afternoon watching the passersby.

Cafeterias are middle-range eateries, common on the seafront in the resorts, usually offering a selection of *platos combinados* (combination dishes), such as a pork chop and fries, or squid and salad, with bread and a drink included.

Restaurantes proper are pretty much the same as back home; they are usually only open for lunch and dinner, and close one day a week. They may offer a menú del día which will be cheaper than ordering à la carte. A restaurant calling itself a *marisquería* specializes in shellfish and seafood, while an *asador* is the place for roast meats. A *venta* is a small, family-run restaurant serving down-to-earth country fare, and is well worth looking out for if you venture away from the coast.

First-time visitors to Spain are often surprised by the late eating hours; the Spanish rarely sit down to lunch (*almuerzo*) before 2pm, and dinner (*cena*) starts around 9:30

---

or 10pm. However, in the resort areas many restaurants stay open all through the day. Although service is included in the bill, it is customary to leave an additional tip (about 10 percent).

WHAT TO EAT

Breakfast: The traditional Spanish breakfast generally consists of *churros y chocolate* (doughnut-like fritters and thick, sweet drinking chocolate) taken standing up at the counter in a café or roadside *kiosko*. Alternatively, try a *tostada con aceite* (toasted roll with olive oil) washed down with *café con leche* (milky coffee). Spanish espresso (*café solo*) is strong stuff, even with a touch of milk (*un cortado*). Resort hotels often offer a full buffet breakfast and, of course, a full English breakfast isn't hard to find.

Tapas: Every good bar offers a selection of tapas. Among the dozens of items to choose from, you may find sweet red peppers in olive oil seasoned with garlic, Russian salad, slices of sausage (both spicy *chorizo* and paprika-flavored *salchichón), jamón serrano* (cured ham), marinated mussels, baby squid, clams, or *tortilla Española* (Spanish omelette, with potato and onion filling, usually served cold in slices). For a larger serving of any given tapa, ask for a *ración*. If you feel that's too much for you, order a *media-ración*.

Vegetable Dishes: The Spanish usually eat vegetables as a first course, rather than as an accompanying dish. But whatever you do, don't miss that great specialty of Andalucía, *alcachofas a la Montilla* — tender artichoke leaves cooked in a mixture of wine and beef broth, thickened with flour and seasoned with mint, garlic, and saffron. *Judías verdes con salsa de tomate*, green beans in tomato sauce, laced with garlic, can also be very good.

Soups: Andalucía's most famous specialty is the cold soup known as *gazpacho*. There are dozens of ways to make it, but the version you are likely to find in southern Spain is a creamy chilled blend of cucumber, tomato, onion, and crushed garlic, with freshly diced green pepper, tomato, and cucumber, chopped hard-boiled egg, and fried croutons on the side.

Originally from Málaga, *ajo blanco* (white garlic soup) is a variation on the more common gazpacho theme. Ground almonds and garlic form the base of this summer refresher, served ice-cold with a garnish of almonds and grapes.

Be sure to try the mixed fish or shellfish soups, *sopa de pescado* and *sopa de mariscos*. Like its French counterpart, the Mediterranean bouillabaisse, *sopa marinera,* is based on the day's catch and seasoned with tomato, onion, garlic, and a dash of white wine or brandy.

Egg Dishes: Egg dishes make popular starters, and a whole Spanish omelette is a filling lunch on its own. *Tortillas* (omelettes) may be filled with asparagus, tuna, or mushrooms. *Huevos a la flamenca* is a baked dish of eggs cooked on a base of tomato, garlic, and herbs — usually accompanied by diced ham or spicy chorizo sausage, fresh peas, and sweet red peppers.

Paella: Spain's most famous dish, which the Spaniards usually eat at lunchtime, deserves to be discussed separately. The main ingredient is saffron-flavored rice, cooked with olive oil, seafood, and chicken. But every chef has his own variation on this colorful dish that originated in Valencia on Spain's eastern coast. The secret of perfect paella is fresh ingredients; fresh seafood such as *langosta* (spiny lobster), *langostinos* (a kind of large shrimp), *cigalas* (giant prawns or sea crayfish), *gambas* (prawns), mussels, and chicken, peas, sweet peppers, and artichoke hearts, all cooked together slowly as the rice absorbs the juices. It also comes with a meat base, and the name paella derives from the flat, round metal pan in which it is cooked.

Seafood: The seafood you are served in the waterfront restaurants was landed on the beach that very morning by the fishermen whose boats lie hauled up on the sand.

The traditional Torremolinos lunch is sardines skewered on a wooden spike and grilled over a charcoal fire on the beach. This simple but tasty dish is quite simply irresistible and an extremely good value. Squid may be an interesting option, either cooked in its own ink (*calamares en su tin-*

The hot dog of Torremolinos — vendors offer skewers of sardines grilled over a fire.

ta), a spicy dish, or simply dipped in batter and fried, and served with a twist of lemon. *Gambas* and *cigalas* are large juicy prawns — choose your own from the display and have them grilled while you choose your wine. When it's available, the langosta is excellent served hot with butter, or cold with mayonnaise. *Boquerones* (fresh anchovies) and *chanquetes* (whitebait) are tossed in flour and deep-fried whole. *Merluza*, or hake, may be served fried, boiled, or mushroom-stuffed, perhaps with tomatoes and potatoes. *Besugo* (sea bream) is a high-quality fish, brushed with olive oil and simply grilled.

Other common items on the menu may include *pez espa-da* (swordfish), *mero* (sea bass), *bonito* (tuna), and *rape* (monkfish). If you have difficulty deciding what to try, you may want to plump for the *fritura malagueña*, a mixed fish fry that includes all of the above seafood. Be warned, though, many of these delicacies are priced on the menu for a 100-gram (approximately ¼-pound) portion; so what appears to be an inexpensive dish will prove to be very costly when you see the final bill.

Chicken and Meat: Spanish chicken is delicious, whether fried, roasted, or braised in white wine or sherry with almonds. The staple *arroz con pollo* (chicken with rice) is tasty.

Many traditional meat dishes make use of offal such as tripe, brains, and sweetbreads. *Riñones al Jerez*, kidneys sautéed with sherry, or *rabo de toro*, braised oxtail served in a rich tomato sauce with carrots and spices, are typical of Andalucía. *Ternera a la Sevillana*, veal in a sherry sauce with green olives, is a specialty of Sevilla. Rabbit (*conejo*) or hare (*liebre*) in white wine forms the basis of many a tasty casserole. Steak and various cuts of beef are also available. A local variation on this international standard is *bistec a la mantequilla de anchoas* (beefsteak with an anchovy butter sauce).

Cheese and Dessert: Spaniards eat cheese (*queso*) after the main course, notably the tangy *queso de manchego,* and the milder *queso de Burgos.* You may also come across *queso de cabrales*, a combination cheese made from goat's, cow's, and sheep's milk in the northwestern province of Asturias. After aging, it becomes blue-veined, and has a sharp taste similar to Roquefort. *Idiázabal* is a smoked and cured goat's cheese.

Fruits in season include *uvas* (grapes), *higos* (figs), *melón* (melon), *naranjas* (oranges), *melocotón* (peaches), *chirimoyas* (custard apples), *fresas* (strawberries), and *cerezas* (cherries). Besides ice cream, southern Spain offers

Most Spanish bodegas — and there are many — offer a sampling of their wines at the end of a winery tour.

pastries and cream desserts in abundance. One appealing preparation is *brazo de gitano*, a rolled sponge cake with rum-flavored cream filling. The ubiquitous *flan*, or egg custard with caramel sauce, appears on menus all over Spain. Eggs cooked with sugar make a thickened custard called *natillas*.

Wine and Spirits: The white wines of Rioja, dry or sweet, are considered quite drinkable, but Rioja reds are the glory of Spain; the aged Gran Reservas (at least five years old) are comparable to some of France's noblest red wines, though Riojas have a character all of their own. Labels to look out for include Marqués de Riscal, Siglo, CUNE, Berberana, and Campo Viejo.

Navarra, north of the Ebro valley, also produces some interesting red wines (look for Campanas, Señorio de Sarría, and Murchante). From La Mancha, between Madrid and Andalucía, come Valdepeñas wines, which are light, crisp, and pleasing to the palate, and serve as a staple for Sangria.

Reds and whites from Catalonia will also appear on wine lists. Labels to look for include Torres and Rene Barbier. Many restaurants have their own inexpensive table wine (*vino de la casa*) that can prove to be a less expensive, but still acceptable alternative. Spain also boasts a mass-produced sparkling wine, referred to as *cava*, which may be rather sweet for northern palates. One of the better brands is Cordorniu.

Sangría, the iced combination of red wine and brandy with lemon, orange, and apple slices, makes a great refresher.

An aristocrat among wines, *Jerez* (sherry) is grown in the chalky vineyards around Jerez de la Frontera. It is aged in casks by blending the young wine with a transfusion of mature sherry, a method known as *solera*. *Fino*, the driest of sherries, is a light, golden aperitif that should be served chilled. A type of fino, called *manzanilla*, is slightly richer; Sanlúcar de Barrameda manzanilla is especially good. *Amontillado*, usually medium dry, is a deeper gold in color, and is heavier than a true fino. *Amoroso* is medium sweet, with an amber color, and *oloroso* is still more full-bodied. Cream sherries are not popular in Spain.

The Andalucían region produces several other semi-sweet to sweet wines, most notably the sweet, mahogany-colored wine of Málaga, called *Málaga Dulce* (rather like port), and the wines of Montilla-Moriles, near Córdoba.

Spanish brandy, or *coñac*, tends to be heavy, but it is usually drinkable and reasonably priced. The more expensive brands are much smoother.

To Help You Order

Could we have a table?	¿nos puede dar una mesa?
Do you have a set menu?	¿tiene un menú del día?
I'd like a/an/some …	quisiera …

beer	**una cerveza**	milk	**leche**
bread	**pan**	mineral water	**agua mineral**
coffee	**un café**	napkin	**una servilleta**
cutlery	**los cubiertos**	potatoes	**patatas**
dessert	**un postre**	rice	**arroz**
fish	**pescado**	salad	**una ensalada**
fruit	**fruta**	sandwich	**un bocadillo**
glass	**un vaso**	sugar	**azúcar**
ice cream	**un helado**	tea	**un té**
meat	**carne**	(iced) water	**agua (fresca)**
menu	**la carta**	wine	**vino**

… and Read the Menu

aceitunas	olives	**judías**	beans
albóndigas	meatballs	**lenguado**	sole
almejas	baby clams	**mariscos**	shellfish
atún	tunny (tuna)	**mejillones**	mussels
bacalao	cod	**ostras**	oysters
besugo	sea bream	**pastel**	cake
calamares	squid	**pimiento**	sweet red pepper
callos	tripe		
cangrejo	crab	**pulpitos**	baby octopus
cerdo	pork	**salchichón**	salami
champiñones	mushrooms	**salmonete**	red mullet
chuletas	chops	**salsa**	sauce
cordero	lamb	**ternera**	veal
entremeses	hors-d'œuvres	**trucha**	trout
huevos	eggs	**uvas**	grapes

HANDY TRAVEL TIPS

An A–Z Summary of Practical Information

A

ACCOMMODATIONS *(hotel; alojamiento)* (see also CAMPING, YOUTH HOSTELS, TOURIST INFORMATION, and RECOMMENDED HOTELS AND RESTAURANTS)

Those traveling independently will find a wide range of accommodations in the Costa del Sol. For a comprehensive listing of accommodations and rates throughout Spain, consult the *Guía Oficial de Hoteles*, available from the Spanish National Tourist Office and some local bookshops.

By law, room rates must be posted in every hotel's reception area and rooms. Meals (including breakfast) are not usually included in this rate, and VAT (IVA in Spanish) will be added to your bill.

Establishments are graded by each of Spain's 17 autonomous governments according to the following system, with one of the following classifications plus a starred rating, depending on the depth and quality of services offered:

Hotel (H): Rated between one and five stars. The most expensive option, topped only by Hotel 5-star Gran Lujo (G.L.), signifying absolutely top-of-the-line accommodations.

Hotel Residencia (HR): Same as a hotel, but there is no restaurant.

Motel (M): Very similar to a hotel, but in reality these accommodations are few and far between.

Hotel Apartamentos (HA): Apartments within hotels, and rated the same as a hotel.

Residencia Apartamentos (RA): Residential apartments without a restaurant, rated the same as a hotel.

Hostal (Hs): A more modest hotel, often family-owned and operated, and rated between one and three stars. Rates overlap with the lower range of hotels, e.g., a three-star *hostal* usually costs about the same as a one- or two-star hotel.

Hostal Residencia (HsR): Similar to a hostal, but without a restaurant.

Pensión (P): A boarding house, rated between one and three stars, with only basic amenities.

Costa del Sol & Andalucía

Fonda (F): A small inn, fairly inexpensive, clean and unpretentious.

Casa de Huéspedes (CH): A guesthouse. Bottom of the scale, but usually clean and comfortable as well as cheap.

Ciudad de Vacaciones (CV): A hotel complex complete with sports facilities.

Casa Rural: Country house offering bed-and-breakfast or self-catering accommodations.

Parador: A state-run hotel, often housed in a castle or other historic building. These hotels are of special interest to motorists, since they are generally located outside towns and in rural areas. Advance booking is not essential, but is highly recommended. For information and bookings in the USA and Canada, contact Marketing Ahead, 433 Fifth Avenue, New York, NY; Tel. 800-223-1356 or (212) 686-9213; fax (212) 686-0271; mahrep@aol.com. In Spain, contact the Paradores de Turismo, Central de Reservas, Requena, 3, 28013 Madrid; Tel. (91) 516 66 66; fax (91) 516 66 57; in the U.K.; Tel. (171) 402-8181; fax (171) 724-9503.

I'd like a single/double room with bath/shower.	**Quisiera una habitación sencilla/doble con baño/ducha.**
What's the rate per night?	**¿Cuál es el precio por noche?**

AIRPORTS (*aeropuerto*) (see also GETTING THERE)
The Costa del Sol is served by Málaga's **Aeropuerto Internacional**, Tel. (95) 224 00 00, situated some 8 km (5 miles) west of the center of Málaga, and 7 km (4 ½ miles) from Torremolinos. There is a bus service every 20 minutes to Málaga, Torremolinos, and Benalmádena-Costa, as well as a half-hourly train service (follow the signs marked *ferrocarril*) to central Málaga and the coastal resorts from Torremolinos to Fuengirola. Taxis can be found at the taxi rank outside the terminal. The journey from the airport to central Málaga or Torremolinos takes about 10 to 15 minutes, and about 20 minutes to Fuengirola.

Other airports with international flights that serve the region are at Gibraltar; Tel. (350) 73026, and Sevilla's San Pablo; Tel. (95) 444 90

00. Buses operate between the latter and the Puerta de Jerez, directly in front of the impressive Hotel Alfonso XIII.

B

BICYCLE AND MOPED RENTAL/HIRE *(bicicletas/ velomotores de alquiler)*

Bicycles can be rented in most places on a daily or weekly basis.
Rates for mopeds are considerably higher. Insurance is obligatory
and costs extra, and a deposit will also be required. A special motor-
bike permit is needed for machines of over 50cc, and the wearing of
crash helmets is compulsory.

I'd like to hire a bicycle.	**Quisiera alquilar una bicicleta.**
What's the charge per day/week?	**¿Cuánto cobran por día/semana?**

BUDGETING FOR YOUR TRIP

To give you an idea of what to expect, here's a list of some average
prices in pesetas. They can only be approximate, however, as prices
vary from place to place, and inflation in Spain, as elsewhere, creeps
up relentlessly. Prices quoted may be subject to IVA, at variable rates.

Accommodations: Rates for a double room can range from as low
as 4,000 to 5,000 ptas (€24.04 to 30.05) at a pensión or hostal to as
much as 60,000 to 70,000 ptas (€360.61 to 420.71) at a top-of-the-
line 5-star hotel. As a rule of thumb, a nice 4-star hotel will cost between 15,000 and 20,000 ptas (€90.15 to 120.20). Beware, though,
some hotels may have three or four pricing seasons. In Sevilla during the Easter Week celebrations and the subsequent Fería de Abril,
for example, rates can double.

Car Rental: Prices vary dramatically depending on whether you rent
before your trip starts; whether you rent from a company in your own
country or locally; how long you rent; whether you want an automatic or manual transmission vehicle; and what insurance coverage you

want, or are obliged, to purchase. If you want a small, manual transmission car for primarily local use, then it may be cheaper to ren from a small company on the Costa del Sol. However, if you live ir North America and are planning on driving extensively or require a car with automatic transmission, then **Auto Europe**, Tel. 888-223-5555, will invariably offer the best rates.

Entertainment: A movie ticket costs 600 ptas (€3.61), a flamenco nightclub (entry and first drink) starts at 3,000 ptas (€18.03), and a discotheque from 1,000 ptas (€6.01). Amusement parks cost 4,000 ptas per adult (€24.04) or 3,000 ptas per child (€18.03)per day. A bullfight ranges from 3,000 to 15,000 ptas (€18.03 to 90.15).

Meals and Drinks: These vary considerably. In a bar, a Continental breakfast will cost between around 500 ptas (€3.01). The cheapest three-course meal with one drink, a menú del día in a small bar or restaurant, will be around 800 to 900 ptas (€4.81 to 5.41). Dinner in a moderately priced restaurant will be about 3,000 ptas (€18.03) per person, including wine. At the top restaurants, expect to pay 6,000 to 7,000 ptas (€36.06 to 42.07) per person, or more, plus wine.

In a bar, a beer in a small bottle or glass will range from 100 to 150 ptas (€0.60 to 0.90), a coffee from 100 to 150 ptas (€0.60 to 0.90), a Spanish brandy from 250 to 300 ptas (€1.50 to 1.80), a soft drink from 150 ptas (€0.90), and a glass of local wine about 50 ptas (€0.30).

Shopping: Again, prices can vary substantially. By far the cheapest places are the very large hypermarkets like Pryca where, for example, a can of San Miguel beer might cost around 65 ptas (€0.39). In a small corner store or *supermercado* (supermarket) that same beer might cost between 100 to 125 ptas (€0.60 to 0.75), and similar price differentials exist for most other goods.

Sightseeing: Sevilla–Cathedral 700 ptas (€4.21); Alcázar 700 ptas (€4.21); Córdoba–Mezquita 750 ptas (€4.51); and Granada–Alhambra 675 ptas (€4.06); Capilla Real 200 ptas (€1.20). Admission prices for most museums are much more modest.

Sports: Per-day greens fees for golf range from around 7,500 ptas (€45.08) up to as much as 30,000 ptas (€180.30) at the very top courses. Tennis court fees start at 1,000 ptas/hour (€6.01). Horseback riding starts at about 2,000 ptas/hour (€12.02).

Taxis: Taxis are generally inexpensive, with a typical city center ride costing around 400 to 500 ptas (€2.40 to 3.01) on the meter. It's best to establish the rate for a long-distance journey before you depart. There are fixed rates, well displayed, for all destinations from Málaga's international airport.

Train: The *cercanía* (local) line between Málaga and Fuengirola is a fast, clean and inexpensive way to travel along this part of the Costa del Sol. A roundtrip ticket costs 520 ptas (€3.13).

I want to change some pounds/dollars.	**Quiero cambiar libras/dólares.**
Do you accept traveler's checks?	**¿Acepta usted cheque de viajero?**
Can I pay with this credit card?	**¿Puedo pagar con esta tarjeta de crédito?**

C

CAMPING *(camping)* (see also TOURIST INFORMATION)

There are numerous official campsites (campings) along the Costa del Sol and throughout Andalucía. Facilities vary, but most sites have electricity and running water, and many have shops and children's playgrounds. Some even have launderettes and restaurants. Rates depend on the facilities available. For a complete list of campsites, consult the *Guía de Campings*, available from the Spanish National Tourist Office and some local bookshops.

Camping outside of official sites is permitted, provided you obtain permission from the landowner. However, you are not allowed to pitch your tent on tourist beaches, in urban areas, or within 1 km ($^1/_2$ mile) of an official site.

Costa del Sol & Andalucía

May we camp here?	**¿Podemos acampar aquí?**

CAR RENTAL/HIRE *(coches de alquiler)*(see also DRIVING)
Unless you plan to stay in one of the remote parts of the Costa del Sol
or are touring extensively, a car is superfluous to your requirements. In
fact, if you are based at one of the popular resorts or major cities, having
a car is more of a disadvantage than an advantage (it's hard to find places
to park and there's always the possibility that your car will be broken into).

But if you must, rent a car before you go. **Auto Europe**, Tel. 888-
223-5555, is the largest organization operating in North America and
more often than not offers the best rates available (especially if you
require a car with an automatic transmission). Otherwise, there are
numerous car-rental firms operating in the Costa del Sol, including all
the major international companies at the airports and some railway stations, but rates and conditions vary enormously.

CDW insurance coverage should be considered a necessity, and if
your credit card doesn't include it then purchase it from the car rental
company. Theft from cars is rampant in this region, and extra coverage against theft of radio and other car parts and damage caused by
thieves is very reasonable and seriously worth considering.

Normally, you must be over 21 to rent a car, and you will need a
valid driver's license that you have held for at least 12 months, your
passport, and a major credit card — cash deposits are prohibitively
large. Visitors from countries other than the U.S., Canada, and those in
the EU may be expected to present an International Driver's License.

I'd like to rent/hire a car (tomorrow).	**Quisiera alquilar un coche (para mañana).**
for one day/a week	**por un día/una semana**
Please include full insurance coverage.	**Haga el favor de incluir el seguro a todo riesgo.**

CLIMATE

Plenty of hot sunshine and cloudless skies are the rule, not the exception, on the Costa del Sol, and in most parts of Andalucía, too. There

are, nevertheless, seasonal variations worth noting when you choose your vacation time. From June–September, hot days with low humidity are followed by slightly cooler evenings; rain is a rarity. In April, May, and October, daytime temperatures remain quite warm, but it can get cold at night. From November–March, sunshine can still be enjoyed, but may be interrupted by chill winds from the mountains and even rain — on average four to six rainy days a month in winter — so be prepared.

Inland, the climate is different. The triangle between Sevilla, Córdoba, and Granada is the hottest in Europe, with summertime temperatures often well over 100° F. And the presence of the towering Sierra Nevada Mountains near Granada ensures that the city and surrounding area sees snow in the wintertime.

The average monthly temperatures for Málaga are:

	J	F	M	A	M	J	J	A	S	O	N	D
max. °C	16	17	18	20	23	25	28	29	26	23	19	17
min. °C	10	11	12	13	15	18	20	21	19	17	14	11
max. °F	60	62	65	68	73	78	83	83	79	73	66	62
min. °F	50	51	54	56	60	64	68	69	67	62	57	53
sea °C	15	14	15	16	17	21	21	23	21	18	17	14
°F	59	57	59	60	62	69	69	73	69	65	62	57

CLOTHING

From June to September, the days are always hot, and lightweight cotton clothes are the order of the day. During the rest of the year, a light jacket and a raincoat or umbrella will come in handy. Warmer attire will be needed in Granada and the Sierra Nevada during the winter. Respectable clothing should, of course, be worn when visiting churches, although women are no longer expected to cover their heads.

COMPLAINTS

By law, all hotels and restaurants must have official complaint forms *(hoja de reclamaciones)* and produce them on demand. The original of this triplicate document should be sent to the Ministry of Tourism; one copy remains with the establishment involved and one copy is given to you. The very action of asking for the *hoja* may resolve the problem in itself, as the establishment knows that tourism authorities take a serious view of such complaints.

CRIME AND SAFETY

Spain's crime rate has increased in recent years, especially in the cities and some of the larger resorts. Here are a few precautions. Always carry a minimum of cash and keep your passport, traveler's checks, credit cards, and cash in a money belt or, better still, in your hotel safe. Never leave bags unattended, or even out of reach. Lock your car and stow any possessions out of sight in the trunk and never leave anything in your car overnight. All thefts must be reported to the police within 24 hours. You will need a copy of the police report in order to make a claim on your vacation insurance.

As a precaution, photocopy the relevant pages of your passport(s) and airline ticket(s) and keep them in a separate place from the originals. If it is stolen, your consulate should be informed (see EMBASSIES AND CONSULATES).

CUSTOMS *(aduana)* AND ENTRY REQUIREMENTS

Most visitors, including citizens of all EU countries, the U.S., Canada, Ireland, Australia, and New Zealand require only a valid passport — no visa, no health certificate — to enter Spain. British tourists may no longer enter Spain on a visitor's passport — a full passport is required. Visitors from South Africa must have a visa, and the requirements and visa can be obtained from the Spanish Consulate General, 37 Short Market Street, Cape Town, 8001; Tel. (27) 21 422 2415; fax (27) 21 422-2328. They're open Mon–Fri 8am–1:30pm.

Currency Restrictions: Tourists are allowed to bring an unlimited amount of Spanish or foreign currency into the country. On departure you must declare any amount beyond the equivalent of 1,000,000 pesetas.

D

DRIVING

Drive on the right, pass (overtake) on the left. Give way to traffic coming from the right.

Road Conditions: Main roads and motorways are generally very good and improving all the time, secondary roads less so. New bypasses around Málaga and the coastal resorts have vastly improved road conditions on the N-340. The stretch of road between Motril and Almería is still narrow and twisting and plagued with slow-moving trucks.

Rules and Regulations: Speed limits are 50km/h (30mph) in built-up areas, 90-100km/h (55–60mph) on highways, and 120km/h (75mph) on motorways. Note that Spanish drivers tend to sound their horn or flash their headlights when overtaking. The use of seat belts (front and back seats) is *obligatory*. A red warning triangle must be carried. Motorcycle riders and their passengers must wear crash helmets.

Spanish roads are patrolled by the motorcycle police of the Civil Guard *(Guardia Civil)*. They can impose on-the-spot fines for common offenses including speeding, overtaking without flashing your lights, traveling too close to the car in front, and driving with burned-out lights.

Fuel: Service stations are plentiful, but it's a good idea to keep an eye on the gauge in more remote areas like the Alpujarra.

Parking *(aparcamiento)*: Parking regulations are strictly enforced — offending vehicles will be towed away *(grua),* and a hefty fine charged for their return. A yellow-painted curb means parking is prohibited at all times; blue means parking is restricted to certain times. Often, you must pay to park and display a sticker inside your window.

If You Need Help: The Civil Guard is efficient with minor mechanical problems and go out of their way to help you if you have a breakdown. Spanish garages are also efficient, but in tourist areas major repairs may take several days because of heavy workload. Spare parts are readily available for all major makes of cars.

Road Signs: Most of the road signs used in Spain are international pictograms. But here are some written signs you will come across:

Autopista (de peaje)	(Toll) motorway (expressway)
Ceda el paso	Give way (Yield)
Circunvalación	Bypass/ring-road
Curva peligrosa	Dangerous bend
Despacio	Slow
Desviación	Diversion (Detour)
Obras	Road works (Men working)
Peligro	Danger
Prohibido aparcar	No parking
Salida de camiones	Truck exit
Sin plomo	Unleaded gas
Can I park here?	**¿Se puede aparcar aquí?**
Full tank, please, top grade.	**Llénelo, por favor, con super.**
Check the oil/tires/battery.	**Por favor, controle el aceite/ los neumáticos/la batería.**
There's been an accident.	**Ha habido un accidente.**

E

ELECTRICITY

220V/50Hz AC *(corriente eléctrica)* is now standard, but older installations of 125 volts can still be found. Check! An adapter for Continental-style two-pin sockets will be needed; American 110V appliances will also require a transformer.

EMBASSIES AND CONSULATES *(embajadas y consulados)*

Australia: Federico Rubio 14, 41004 Sevilla;Tel. (95) 422 09 71.

Canada: Edificio Horizonte, Calle Cervantes, Málaga; Tel. (95) 222 33 46; Avda. de los Pinos, 34–Casa 4 Mairena del Aljarafe, Sevilla; Tel. (95) 476 88 28.

Republic of Ireland: Avenida de los Boliches 15, Fuengirola; Tel. (95) 247 51 08. Plaza de Santa Cruz, 6-BjA, Sevilla; Tel. (95) 421 63 61.

U.K.: Edificio Duquesa, Calle Duquesa de Parcent 8, Málaga; Tel. (95) 221 75 71; Plaza Nueva 8-B, Sevilla; Tel. (95) 422 88 74.

U.S.: Centro Comercial Las Rampas II, Fuengirola; Tel. (95) 247 48 91. Paseo de Las Delicias, 7, Sevilla; Tel. (95) 423 18 85.

EMERGENCIES (*emergencias*)

Unless you are fluent in Spanish, you should seek help through your hotel receptionist or the local tourist office. If you can speak Spanish, the following telephone numbers may be useful.

	Ambulance	Police	Sea Rescue
Spain	061	091	900202202
Gibraltar	199	199	

G

GETTING THERE (see also AIRPORTS)

By Air

From North America: At the time of writing, only one U.S.-based airline has a direct, scheduled flight to the Costa del Sol and Andalucía, although some charter flights flight directly, with a change of planes in Madrid.

Iberia (Tel. 800-772-4642; web site <www.iberia.com>) has flights from New York City and Miami to Madrid, and connections from there to Málaga, Sevilla, and other smaller airports. Air Europa (Tel. 718-244-7055; fax 718-656-0408; web site <www.air-europa.com>) has flights from New York City to Madrid, and connections from there to Málaga, Sevilla, and other smaller airports. It also has a roundtrip weekly flight between New York City and Málaga. In addition, Spanair (Tel. 888-545-5757 or web site <www.spanair.com>) flies out of

Costa del Sol & Andalucía

Washington, DC and has flights to Madrid with onward connections to Málaga and Sevilla. Spanair also offers the economical Spain Pass, good for travel on the mainland and to the Canary Islands.

From Europe: Scheduled flights link major European cities with Málaga, and charter flights arrive in the hundreds from numerous destinations in northern Europe.

By Car

From the U.K., the main route from the French ferry ports runs south through western France to Bordeaux and into Spain at Irún, west of the Pyrenees. Continue on the A8 to San Sebastián, and then take the N-I all the way to Madrid, via Burgos. Continue through Madrid on the M30 and then take the A4/N-IV south to Bailén. From there, either continue on the N-IV westward to Córdoba and Sevilla, and then on the A4 to Cádiz via Jerez de la Frontera, or take the N-323 south via Jaén to Granada. At Granada, either continue directly south on the N-323 to the coast at Motril, or follow the A92 west and then the N-321 south to Málaga.

Alternatively, take the eastern route through France to Perpignan in the southeast, you can follow the A7 motorway south via Barcelona, Tarragona, Valencia, and Alicante to Murcia. From Murcia continue to Puerto Lumbreras where you can continue on the N-340 to Almería, Málaga, the Costa del Sol, and around the Atlantic coast to Cádiz; or head westward on the N-342/A92 to Guadix, Granada, and then Sevilla.

Your driving time (three steady days with either choice) can be cut by using the long-distance car-ferry service from Plymouth to Santander and Portsmouth to Bilbao in northern Spain. From Santander or Bilbao, follow the road to Burgos and proceed as above.

By Rail

From the U.K., take the high-speed Eurostar train (web site <www.eurostar.com>) from London's Waterloo International Station through the Channel Tunnel to Paris Gare du Nord. French National Railways, SNCF (web site <www.sncf.com>), operates high-speed TGV trains from either Gare Montparnasse or Gare d'Orleans to the French/Spanish border at Hendaye/Irún or Cerbere/Port Bou on the west and east sides of the Pyrenees, respectively. From Irún, change to a Spanish Madrid-bound RENFE train or the direct, but very slow, *Tren Media Luna* to Algeciras. From Port Bou, you'll take a fast TALGO train, continuing on to Madrid either via Zaragoza or Valencia.

Alternatively, take a RENFE hotel train (*hotel tren*) from Paris to Madrid (Francisco de Goya) or Barcelona (Joan Miró). From Madrid (Puerta de Atocha), take either the high-speed AVE train to Córdoba and on to Sevilla, or the fast express T200 service to Córdoba and on to Málaga.

Other international hotel tren services are between Lisbon and Madrid (Lusitania); Milan and Barcelona (Salvador Dalí); and Zurich and Barcelona (Pau Casals).

By Sea
From the U.K., two companies offer car-ferry services to mainland Spain, with schedules varying by the season. Brittany Ferries (Tel. 0870 901 2400) has sailings with an average crossing time of 24 hours between Plymouth and Santander. P&O European Ferries (Tel. 0870 242 4999) has sailings with an average crossing time of 35 hours between Portsmouth and Bilbao. Motorists can then travel on the N-623 from Santander to Burgos and the junction with the N1, and from Bilbao on the A68 to its junction with the A1. From either place, continue south, using the directions in the By Car section above to the Costa del Sol and Andalucía.

GUIDES AND TOURS
English-speaking guides can be hired through local tourist offices (see Tourist Information on page 124). Guided tours and excursions can be booked at most hotels or through any of the numerous travel agencies *(agencia de viaje)*.

HEALTH & MEDICAL CARE
Anything other than basic emergency treatment can be very expensive, and you should not leave home without adequate insurance, prefer-

ably including coverage for an emergency flight home in the event of serious injury or illness.

British and Irish citizens are entitled to free emergency hospital treatment. You should obtain form E111 from a post office before you leave in order to qualify. You may have to pay part of the price of treatment or any medicine you require; keep receipts so that you can claim a refund when you return home.

The main health hazard on the Costa del Sol is also its biggest attraction — the sun. Take along a sun hat, sunglasses, and plenty of high-factor sunscreen, and limit your sunbathing sessions to an hour or less until you begin to tan.

For minor ailments, visit the local first-aid post *(ambulatorio)*. Away from your hotel, don't hesitate to ask the police or a tourist information office for help. At your hotel, ask the staff for assistance. *Farmacias* (pharmacies) are usually open during normal shopping hours. After hours, at least one per town remains open all night. Called a *farmacia de guardia,* its location is posted in the window of all other *farmacias* and in the local newspapers.

Where's the nearest (all-night) pharmacy?	**¿Dónde está la farmacia (de guardia) más cercana?**
I need a doctor/dentist.	**Necesito un médico/dentista.**
sunburn/sunstroke	**quemadura del sol/ una insolación**
an upset stomach	**molestias de estómago**

HOLIDAYS *(días festivos)*

Banks, post offices, government offices, and many other businesses are closed on the following dates. Andalucía celebrates its regional holiday on 28 February. Note that there are also a number of local and regional holidays and saint's days; check with the local tourist office.

1 January	*Año Nuevo*	New Year's Day
6 January	*Epifanía*	Epiphany
19 March	*San José*	St. Joseph's Day

1 May	*Día del Trabajo*	Labor Day
25 July	*Santiago Apóstol*	St. James's Day
15 August	*Asunción*	Assumption Day
12 October	*Día de la Hispanidad*	Columbus Day
1 November	*Todos los Santos*	All Saints' Day
6 December	*Día de la Constitución*	Constitution Day
8 December	*Immaculada Concepción*	Immaculate Conception
25 December	*Día de Navidad*	Christmas Day

Movable dates:

Jueves Santo	Monday–Thursday; late March–late April
Viernes Santo	Good Friday; late May–early June
Corpus Christi	Corpus Christi

LANGUAGE

The national language of Spain, Castilian Spanish, is spoken in the Costa del Sol and Andalucía. Throughout Andalucía, the local dialect Andaluz, which is a little more difficult to understand, is commonly used. English is widely spoken in the resort towns, though it is polite to learn at least a few basic phrases. The *Berlitz Spanish Phrasebook and Dictionary* covers most situations you are likely to encounter, and the *Berlitz Spanish-English/English-Spanish Pocket Dictionary* contains some 12,500 entries, plus a menu-reader supplement.

MEDIA (see also WEB SITES)

Radio and Television *(radio; televisión):* There are several local radio stations, such as Central FM (98.6 and 103.8), Onda Cero Marbella (101.6), Coastline Radio (97.7), Spectrum (105.5), and Premiere Network Radio (96.8 and 107.0) that broadcast in English on the FM band. Radio broadcasts can also be picked up from

Costa del Sol & Andalucía

Gibraltar. Network television programs are all in Spanish, but better hotels and many English bars also have satellite TV with CNN, MTV, Superchannel, Sky TV, etc.

Newspapers and Magazines *(periódico, revista):* In the major tourist areas you can buy most European newspapers on the day of publication, with some English ones even having Spanish editions, but at about three times the price. The *International Herald Tribune* is also widely available as are all kinds of British and American magazines. The weekly *Sur in English,* available free, is aimed at residents on the Costa del Sol and carries local news and events. The *Costa Del Sol News* is another English language newspaper that is published every Thursday. It costs 100 ptas (€0.60) and offers entertainment listings as well as information about religious services in the area. The latter has a particularly useful page called *Costa Fun…What's On and Where to Go* that gives comprehensive and useful information about all the tourist attractions along the Costa del Sol and Gibraltar.

MONEY
Currency: The monetary unit of Spain is the peseta (which is abbreviated pta/ptas).

Coins are found in the following denominations: 1, 5, 10, 25, 50, 100, 200, and 500 pesetas. Besides the fact that they increase in size according to value (and the 25 ptas coin has a hollow center) coins alternate in color according to their value, with the 1 pta being silver and the 5 ptas gold, etc. In 2000, a new, commemorative 2,000 ptas coin was issued.

Banknotes come in 1,000 (green), 2,000 (orange), 5,000 (brown), and 10,000 (blue) ptas.

As of 1 January 2001, the Euro transplants the peseta and becomes the official currency of Spain. Until that date almost all prices in Spain are shown as pesetas followed by Euros, which is how they appear in this guide.

Currency Exchange: Outside of normal banking hours, many travel agencies and other businesses displaying a *cambio* sign will change foreign currency into pesetas. Larger hotels will also change guests' money. The exchange rate is slightly less than at the bank. Traveler's checks always get a better rate than cash. Take your passport with you when changing money or traveler's checks for identification purposes.

ATMs: ATM machines can be found everywhere.

Credit Cards, Traveler's Checks and Eurochecks: These are accepted in most hotels, restaurants, and big shops.

VAT *(IVA)*: Remember that IVA *(impuesto sobre el valor agregado)*, the Spanish equivalent of value added tax, will be added to your hotel and restaurant bills; it currently stands at 7 percent. A higher rate of 16 percent applies to car-rental charges and a rate of 4 percent applies to certain basic necessities.

OPENING HOURS

Shops and offices and other businesses generally observe the after-noon siesta, opening between 9:30 or 10am–1:30 or 2pm, and from 4:30 or 5pm–7:30 or 8pm, but in tourist areas many places now stay open all day. Banks are generally open from 9am–2pm, but beware of the numerous public holidays.

POLICE *(policía)*

There are three separate police forces in Spain. The *Policía Municipal*, who are attached to the local town hall and usually wear blue uniforms, are the ones to whom you should report theft and other crimes. The *Policía Nacional* is a national anti-crime unit wearing dark-blue uniforms; and the *Guardia Civil*, with green uni-forms, is a national force whose most conspicuous role is as a highway patrol. Spanish police, often working in pairs, are generally very courteous and helpful towards foreign visitors.

The emergency number is 911.

POST OFFICES *(correos)*

Post offices handle mail and telegrams only; normally, you cannot make telephone calls from them. Routine postal business is generally transacted from 8:30am–2:30pm, Monday–Friday, and from 9:30am–1pm on Saturday. Postage stamps *(sellos)* are also on sale at tobacconists *(estancos)* and hotel desks, and at tourist shops selling postcards. Mail for destinations outside Spain should be posted in the box marked *extranjero* (overseas), and delivery is slow.

PUBLIC TRANSPORTATION

By Bus *(autobús)*: Buses are an excellent form of transportation, not just along the Costa del Sol and throughout Andalucía. They reach many destinations that the train doesn't, and when they do serve the same destinations, they are more often than not cheaper, faster, and more frequent. Automóviles Portillo, Tel. (95) 224 73 14, operates a service every half-hour from Málaga that connects Torremolinos, Tel. (95) 238 24 19; Benalmádena-Costa, Tel. (95) 244 35 63; Mijas; Fuengirola, Tel. (95) 247 50 66; Marbella, Tel. (95) 277 21 92; San Pedro Alcántara, Tel. (95) 278 13 96; and Estepona, Tel. (95) 280 02 49. Alsina Graells Sur, Tel. (95) 231 82 95, operates daily service between Málaga and Sevilla, Tel. (95) 441 71 11; Granada, Tel. (958) 25 13 50; Córdoba, Tel. (957) 23 64 74; Almería, Tel. (950) 22 18 88; and La Linea de la Concepción, Tel. (956) 10 23 96, a short walk from the border with Gibraltar.

By Ferry *(barco)*: Algeciras is a major port, and Trasmediterránea, Tel. (956) 66 52 00 or web site <www.trasmediterranea.com>, is the largest company operating from there. It has frequent sailings, on high-speed or regular ferries, to Ceuta, Tel. (956) 50 95 52, a Spanish enclave on the Moroccan coast, or Tangier, Morocco, Tel. (09) 941101. It also operates a daily ferry (except Friday from

Málaga) on the much longer routes from Málaga, Tel. (95) 224 39 10, and Almería, Tel. (952)23 61 55, to Melilla, Tel. (952) 68 12 44, the other Spanish enclave on the Moroccan coast. There is also a very limited ferry service between Gibraltar and Tangier.

By Taxi *(taxi)*: Taxis in the major cities have meters, but in villages along the rest of the coast they usually don't, so it's a good idea to check the fare before you get in. If you take a long trip, you will be charged a two-way fare whether you make the return journey or not. By law a taxi may carry only four persons. A green light and/or a *libre* (free) sign indicates that a taxi is available. You can telephone for a cab as well. The numbers to call are as follows: in Benalmádena, Tel. 244 15 45; in Estepona, Tel. 280 29 00; in Fuengirola, Tel. 247 10 00; in Málaga, Tel. 232 79 50; in Marbella, Tel. 277 05 03; in Torremolinos, Tel. 238 06 00; and in Gibraltar, Tel. 70027.

By Train *(tren)*: A suburban (Cercanías) rail service runs along the coast between downtown Málaga (the Centro-Alameda station) and Fuengirola, Tel. (95) 247 85 40. It includes stops at the RENFE train station, the international airport in Málaga, Torremolinos, Tel. (95) 236 02 02, and Benalmádena, Tel. (95) 236 02 02. Trains depart Málaga every thirty minutes between 6am and 10:30pm. From Fuengirola, there is half-hourly service between 6:45am and 11:15pm.

From the mainline (RENFE) station in Málaga, Tel. (95) 236 02 02, there is service to Ronda, Tel. (95) 287 16 73, and on to Algeciras. From Córdoba (Tel. (957) 40 02 02), Granada (Tel. (958) 27 12 72), and Sevilla Santa Justa (Tel. (95) 454 02 02), there are connections to other destinations in Andalucía. There are also long-distance (*largo recorrido*) trains via Córdoba to Madrid (and on to Zaragoza, Burgos, and Bilbao) and from Barcelona via Valencia or Madrid and Zaragoza. Timetables and information are available from railway stations and tourist offices, and from the RENFE web site <www.renfe.es>.

Costa del Sol & Andalucía

Train Passes: For information on the Spain Flexipass, Spain Rail 'n Drive Pass, point-to-point rail tickets on Spanish trains, including the high-speed Euromed (Barcelona, Valencia, Alicante) or AVE (Madrid, Córdoba, Sevilla, Cádiz, Málaga) trains, contact Rail Europe at Tel. 888-382-7245 or web site <www.raileurope.com>, *before* you leave for Europe. The web site also contains useful rail trip planning information, especially the section on fares and schedules.

The Spain Flexipass gives you three days of unlimited rail travel (in 1st or 2nd class) starting at US$155 (2nd class). Additional rail days are US$30 (2nd class) and US$35 (1st class) each. The Spain Rail 'n Drive Pass gives you three days of unlimited rail travel plus two days of car rental. Prices depend on class of rail travel and car category (four categories are available) and start at US$255 per person for two traveling together.

Where is the (nearest) bus stop?	**¿Dónde está la parada de autobuses (más cercana)?**
When's the next bus/boat for…?	**¿A qué hora sale el próximo autobús/barco para…?**
I want a ticket to…	**Quiero un billete para…**
single (one-way)	**ida**
return (round-trip)	**ida y vuelta**
Will you tell me when to get off?	**¿Podría indicarme cuándo tengo que bajar?**

RELIGION

Spain is a Roman Catholic country. However, mass in English is conducted in Benalmádena-Costa at the Virgen del Carmen (Sol y Mar) every Sunday and feast day at 10am and at Los Boliches in the St. Andrew's Chapel, Edif. Jupiter, Avda. Jesús Santos Rein, every Saturday at 5:45pm. Many other Protestant denominations such as the Church of England (Episcopal), the Church of Scotland

(Presbyterian), and the Methodist church are represented on the Costa del Sol. In addition, there are congregations of Christian Scientists, Jehovah's Witnesses, and Mormons here. In Málaga, Marbella and Fuengirola, Moslem mosques can be found, and in Marbella and Torremolinos, there is a concentration of Jewish synagogues. For services, refer to *Sur in English*, page 2, or contact the local tourist office.

TELEPHONE (*teléfono*)

The country code for Spain is 34. To reach an international operator from Spain, dial 025.

The country code for the U.S. and Canada is 1; for Great Britain 44; for Australia 61; for New Zealand 64; for the Republic of Ireland 353; and for South Africa 27.

In addition to the telephone office, Telefonica, in Málaga and other major towns and cities, there are phone booths everywhere from which you can make local and international calls. Instructions in English and area codes for different countries are displayed in the booths. International calls are expensive, so be sure to have a plentiful supply of 100 ptas coins. Some telephones accept credit cards, and many require a phone card (*tarjeta telefónica*), available from a tobacconist. For international direct dialing, pick up the receiver, wait for the dial tone, then dial 07. Wait for a second tone and then dial the country code, followed by the area code (minus the initial zero) and number.

Remember, calling directly from your hotel room is almost always prohibitively expensive unless you are using a calling card. Your long-distance carrier should have a free connection number you can dial for access. Be sure to determine what it is before you depart your home country, since the number is different for each country and is often difficult to obtain once you are in the Costa del Sol.

Can you get me this number? **¿Puede comunicarme con este número?**

Costa del Sol & Andalucía

TIME ZONES

Spanish time coincides with most of Western Europe — Greenwich Mean Time plus one hour. In summer, another hour is added for daylight saving time.

New York	London	**Spain**	Sydney	Auckland
6am	11am	**noon**	8pm	10pm

TIPPING

Since a service charge is normally included in hotel and restaurant bills, tipping is not obligatory. However, about 10 percent of the bill is usual for taxi drivers, bartenders, and waiters. It's also appropriate to tip bellboys, bullfight ushers, and others offering personal services.

TOILETS *(baños, sanitarios)*

There are many expressions for "toilets" in Spanish: *aseos, servicios, WC, water*, and *retretes*; the first two are the most common. Just about every bar and restaurant has a toilet available for public use. It is, though, polite to buy a drink in the bar. The usual signs are *Damas* for women, and *Caballeros* for men, though you might occasionally see *Señoras* and *Señores*.

TOURIST INFORMATION *(oficina de turismo)*

Information may be obtained from one of the international branches of the Spanish National Tourist Office, as listed below.

Australia: Level 2–203 Castlereagh Street, NSW, 2000 Sydney South, Tel. (2) 2647966.

Canada: 2 Bloor Street West, 34th Floor, Toronto, Ontario M4W 3E2; Tel. 416-961-3131; fax 416-961-1992; email <spainto@globalserve.net>.

U.K.: 22-23 Manchester Square, London, W1M 5AP; Tel. (0171) 486-8077; fax (0171) 486-8034; email <buzon.oficial@londres.oet.mcx.es>.

U.S.: Water Tower Place, Suite 915 East, 845 N. Michigan Avenue, Chicago, IL 60611; Tel. 312-642-1992; fax 312- 642-9817; email <buzon.oficial@chicago.oet.mcx.es>

8383 Wilshire Boulevard, Suite 960, Beverly Hills, Los Angeles, CA 90211; Tel. 213-658-7188; fax 323-658-1061; email <buzon .oficial@losangeles.oet.mcx.es>. 665 Fifth Avenue, New York, NY 10103; Tel. 212-265-8822; fax 212-265-8864; email <buzon.oficial@nuevayork.oet.mcx.es>. 1221 Brickell Avenue, Miami, FL 33131; Tel. 305-358-1992; fax 305- 358-8223; email <buzon.oficial@miami.oet.mcx.es>.

For more detailed information about the Costa del Sol, contact the Costa del Sol Patronato de Turismo, Palacio de Congresos Costa del Sol, Calle México, s/n, 29620 Torremolinos, Málaga, Tel. (95) 205 86 94/95/96; fax (95) 205 03 11; email <costadelsol@ sopde.es>; web site <www.costadelsol.sopde.es>. For more detailed information about Gibraltar, contact the Gibraltar Information Bureau, Duke of Kent House, Cathedral Square, Tel. (350) 45000 or fax 74943.

For more detailed information about Andalucía, contact the Consejería de Turismo y Deporte Turismo Andaluz, S.A., Centro Internacional de Turismo Andalucía (CINTA), Ctra. 340, Km. 189.6, 29600 Marbella, Málaga; Tel. (95) 283 87 85; fax (95) 283 63 69; email <promocion@turismo-andaluz>; web site <www.Andalucía.org>.

For more detailed information about individual cities and towns in Andalucía and along the Costa del Sol, visit the local tourist office (*oficina de turismo*). Offices are normally open from 9am–1pm and 4–7pm, and all of them will have somebody on staff who will be able to give advice and information in English.

W

WEB SITES (see also ACCOMMODATIONS, GETTING THERE, PUBLIC TRANSPORTATION, and TOURIST INFORMATION)
The English-language publications *Sur in English* and *Costa del Sol News* have web sites that provide information about special events for visitors. Check out <www.surinenglish.com> and <www.ctv.es/cbnews/solnews.htm>. For general tourist information, look at <www.tourspain.es>.

WEIGHTS AND MEASURES
Spain uses the metric system.

Costa del Sol & Andalucía

Length

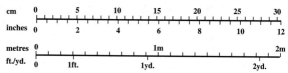

Weight

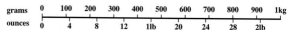

Temperature

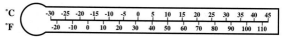

Fluid measures

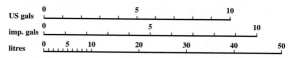

Distance

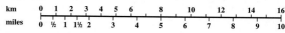

YOUTH HOSTELS *(albergues de juveniles)* (see also
ACCOMMODATIONS, CAMPING, and WEB SITES)
Red de Albergues Juveniles de Andalucía provides a complete listing
of all hostels on the Costa del Sol and in Andalucía on their web site
<www.inturjoven.com>.

Note that the Spanish word *hostal* does not mean youth hostel, but
a basic hotel.

Recommended Hotels

The following hotels, covering the Costa del Sol and Andalucía, are listed alphabetically by region and by name. After each hotel's name, its Spanish hotel grade (see ACCOMMODATIONS on page 103 for an explanation) appears, followed by its price category. Wheelchair accessibility is not that common in Spain. Although one or two smaller hotels may cater to the handicapped, as a rule of thumb, it is generally the larger and more expensive properties that may have such facilities. Check with a particular hotel when booking if you must have such facilities.

To indicate each hotel's price category, we have used the symbols below, which are based on the rate for a double room with bath or shower during the high season. Low season rates can be considerably lower. Please note that these rates do not include breakfast.

$	below 10,000 ptas (€60.01)
$$	10,000 - 15,000 ptas; (€60.01 - 90.02)
$$$	15,000 - 20,000 ptas; (€90.02 - 120.02)
$$$$	20,000 - 30,000 ptas; (€120.02 - 180.03)
$$$$$	30,000 - 50,000 ptas; (€180.03 - 300.51)
$$$$$$	over 50,000 ptas (€300.51)

Cádiz

Hotel Puertatierra (4 stars) $$ *Avda. de Andalucía, 34; Tel. (956) 27 21 11; fax 25 03 11.* Beautifully designed modern hotel with a fine location, close to both the beach and old town. All expected amenities including on-site parking. 98 rooms. Major credit cards.

Carmona

Hotel Casa Palacio Casa de Carmona (5 stars) $$$$ *Plaza de Lasso, 1; Tel. (95) 414 33 00; fax 414 37 52; web site <www.casadecarmona.com>.* A 16th-century palace carefully and lovingly renovated into a beautiful and very hospitable luxury hotel. Every room is unique, and filled with handpicked antiques from Madrid, London, and Paris. 33 rooms. Major credit cards.

Ceuta

Parador "Hotel La Muralla" (4 stars) $$$ *Plaza Ntra. Sra. De África, 15; Tel. (956) 51 49 40; fax 51 49 47.* Views to the north to Gibraltar and south over Morocco, nice gardens, and pool. Built into the ancient palace walls. 106 rooms. Major credit cards.

Córdoba

Hotel NH Amistad Córdoba (4 stars) $$$ *Plaza Maimó-nides, 3; Tel. (957) 42 03 35; fax 42 03 65.* Located in the Jewish quarter close to the Mezquita. Two 18th-century mansions, next to the old Moorish wall, combined and restored to create a fully modernized hotel in harmony with this historic city. 84 rooms. Major credit cards.

Hotel Macía Alfaros (4 stars) $$$ *c/. Alfaros, 18; Tel. (957) 49 19 20; fax 49 22 10, e-mail* <alfaros@igm.es>. In the heart of the city, this is a dignified oasis of calm in the old quarter. Moorish in style, it has elegant and fully equipped rooms, a pool, restaurants, and private parking. 135 rooms. Major credit cards.

Hotel Selu (3 stars) $$ *Eduardo Dato, 7; Tel. (957) 47 65 00; fax 47 83 76.* In the commercial and historic center, close to the historic quarter and train and bus stations. Modern facilities and gym. 115 rooms. Major credit cards.

El Peurto de Santa María

Hotel Monasterio San Miguel (4 stars) $$$$ *c/. Larga, 27; Tel. (956) 54 04 40; fax 54 26 04.* An intriguing complex originally constructed in the 18th century as a Capuchin convent. These days, the cells and other rooms have been beautifully renovated in Classical style to create an outstandingly interesting hotel. Previous guests include the Spanish royal family. 160 rooms. Major credit cards.

El Rocío

Hotel Toruño (2 stars) $$ *Plaza del Acebuchal, 22; Tel. (959) 44 23 23; fax 44 23 38.* A delightful modern hotel in this historic and most unusual small town. Views over the marshes of Doñana and the array of wildlife inhabiting it. 30 rooms. Major credit cards.

Estepona

Las Dunas Beach Hotel & Spa (5 star GL) $$$$$ *Ctra. Cádiz, Km 163.5; Tel. (95) 279 43 45; fax 279 48 25; web site* <www.las-dunas.com>. A low-rise Andalucían-style hacienda with Moorish influences. Soothing color schemes inside and out; sub-tropical gardens leading to the beach; sports, and health club. Luxurious rooms with terraces or sun decks offering marvelous views. 73 rooms. Major credit cards.

Kempinski Resort Hotel (5 star) $$$$$ *Ctra. de Cádiz, Km 159; Tel. (95) 280 95 00; fax 280 95 50; web site* <www.kempinski-spain.com>. Opened in September 1999. The rooms in this architecturally interesting hotel all have sea views. There are also sub-tropical gardens, a 1-km (1/2-mile) beach, numerous pools, water sports, horseback riding, a restaurant serving haute cuisine, and the *Polly Vital* wellness center. 149 rooms. Major credit cards.

Hotel La Cartuja $$$ *Campos de la Cartuja, Ctra. Benahavis, km 1.5; Tel. (95) 288 22 70; fax 288 20 86.* A very stylish hotel, both in terms of its architecture and furnishings, overlooking the Atalaya golf course just inland from the sea. Offers an array of self-catering suites, pools, sports facilities, and a fine restaurant. Major credit cards.

Fuengirola

Hotel El Puerto (3 stars) $$ *Paseo Maritimo, 32; Tel. (95) 247 01 00; fax 247 01 66*. An attractive new circular hotel set on a prime location on the promenade at Fuengirola. Pleasant rooms and a rooftop pool with spectacular views over the Costa del Sol. 300 rooms. Major credit cards.

Gibraltar

The Rock Hotel (5 stars) $$$ *Europa Road; Tel. (350) 73000; fax 73513*. Traditional English style hotel and restaurant with sweeping views over the bay and Strait of Gibraltar and Africa on the horizon. Nine-acre garden with a saltwater pool. 104 rooms. Major credit cards.

Granada

Alhambra Palace (4 stars) $$$ *Peña Partida, 2; Tel. (958) 22 14 68; fax 22 64 04*. An impressive and elaborate Moorish-style palace in the Alhambra Park complex. It has stunning hill-top views over the city and up to the Sierra Nevada. 144 rooms. Major credit cards.

Parador San Francisco (4 stars) $$$$ *Real de la Alhambra, s/n; Tel. (958) 22 14 40; fax 22 22 64*. Set within the precincts of the Alhambra and housed in the 15th-century convent where Queen Isabella was originally interred. 46 rooms. Major credit cards.

Hotel Carmen (4 stars) $$$ *Acera del Darro, 62; Tel. (958) 25 83 00; fax 25 64 62*. Modern hotel in the city center close to the monuments. Full facilities, including restaurant, bar, pool, and parking lot. 283 rooms. Major credit cards.

Hotel Palacio de Santa Inés (3 stars) $$$$ *Cuesta de Santa Inés, 9; Tel. (958) 22 23 62; fax 22 24 65*. A 16th-century palace once known as the House of the Eternal Father that has been beautifully converted into a hotel of considerable charm. Situated in the historic Albaicin area opposite to the towering Alhambra fortress. 6 rooms; 6 suites. Major credit cards.

Maciá Gran Vía (3 stars) $$ *Gran Vía de Colón, 25; Tel. (958) 28 54 64; fax 28 55 91.* A very pleasant modern hotel conveniently located on the middle of the city's main street and just a few minutes' walk from the cathedral. Underground garage. 85 rooms. Major credit cards.

Hotel Guadalupe (3 stars) JJ *Avda. los Alixares, s/n; Tel. (958) 22 34 23; fax 22 37 98.* Situated in the Alhambra complex very close to the monument, this is a comfortable hotel with a Granadino style ambience. 58 rooms. Major credit cards.

Guadix

Hotel Comercio (2 stars) $ *Avda. Mariana Pineda, 65; Tel. (958) 66 15 00; fax 66 01 79.* A short distance from the town center and the intriguing Barrio Santiago. Recently totally modernized, it has very comfortable, oversized rooms and an excellent restaurant. 24 rooms. Major credit cards.

Guillena

Hotel Cortijo Águila Real (4 stars) $$$ *Ctra. de Guillena to Burguillos, Km 4; Tel. (95) 578 50 06; fax 578 43 30.* A classically traditional ranch, just 15 minutes from the center of Sevilla. Beautifully converted rooms around the main yard, fine restaurant, inviting pool, and a small bullring. 12 rooms. Major credit cards.

Jerez de la Frontera

Hotel Jerez (4 stars) $$$ *Avda. Alcalde Álvaro Domecq, 35; Tel. (956) 30 06 00; fax 30 50 01; web site <www.hoteljerez .com>.* Elegantly designed hotel in a residential area that's just a few minutes' walk from all attractions. Large modern rooms, beautiful pool and gardens, and sports facilities.

Hotel Guadalete (4 stars) $$$ *Avda. Duque de Abrantes, 50; Tel. (956) 18 22 88; fax 18 22 93.* Named after the famous battle, this charming hotel is set in its own spacious grounds next to the Royal Equestrian school. It has an unusual mixture, but one that works well, of Jerez and British decor. 125 rooms. Major credit cards.

Malaga

Hotel Larios (4 stars) $$$ *c/. Larios, 2; Tel. (95) 222 22 00; fax 222 24 07; web site* <www.info@hotel-larios.com>. In the main shopping center by a pleasant square, the building dates from the turn of the century. Completely renovated four years ago, it now has a modern Art Deco design and a dignified ambience. 40 rooms. Major credit cards.

Hotel NH Málaga (4 stars) $$$ *Avda. Rio Guadalmedina, s/n; Tel. (95) 207 13 23.* Opened in 1999, this has a grand location just outside the old part of town. Impressive modern rooms, pleasant public areas, and private parking. 133 rooms. Major credit cards.

Parador Málaga-Gibralfaro (4 stars) $$$$ *Castillo de Gibralfaro, s/n; Tel. (95) 222 19 02; fax 222 19 04.* A small parador-grade accommodation beside the Moorish castle on the hilltop above the city. Grand views over the city and the bay. 38 rooms. Major credit cards.

Hotel Don Curro (3 stars) $$$ *c/. Sancha de Lara, 7; Tel. (95) 222 72 00; fax 221 59 46.* Established hotel with a very central location. All rooms with private bath and modern facilities. 120 rooms. Major credit cards.

Marbella

Gran Meliá Don Pepe (5 stars) $$$$$ *c/. José Meliá, s/n; Tel. (95) 277 03 00; fax 277 99 54; web site* <www.solmelia .es>. An imposing hotel just a 5-minute walk from the city center. Only tropical gardens and pools separate it from the beach. Every expected luxury can be found here, plus a sports club with Jacuzzi and sauna, and renowned restaurants. 202 rooms. Major credit cards.

Don Carlos Beach & Golf Resort Hotel (5 stars) $$$$$ *Ctra. de Cádiz, Km 192; Tel. (95) 283 11 40; fax 283 34 29.* Set in subtropical gardens on one of the best beaches on the coast. Totally renovated in 1997 with every possible luxury, views of Gibraltar and Africa, restaurants, bars, tennis, and golf. 240 rooms. Major credit cards.

Chapas Palacio del Sol (3 stars) $$$ *Ctra. Cádiz, Km 192; Tel. (95) 283 13 75; fax 283 13 77.* Vacation complex set amid pine trees beside the beach about 8 km (5 miles) east of town. Water sports facilities. 320 rooms. Major credit cards.

Rincón de la Victoria

Hotel de Campo Molino de Santillana (2 stars) JJ *Ctra. de Macharaviaya, Km 3; Tel. (95) 211 57 80; fax 21 57 82.* A charming, small cortijo-style hotel east of Málaga in the Axarquía region. Set in its own grounds surrounded by almond, olive, and fruit orchards, with vistas over the Mediterranean below. Fine restaurant. 10 rooms. Major credit cards.

Ronda

Hotel Reina Victoria (4 stars) $$$ *c/. Jerez, 25; Tel. (95) 287 12 40; fax 287 10 75; e-mail* reinavictoriaronda@husa.es. Dating from 1906, but renovated to include all modern facilities, this sits in its own gardens and has panoramic views over the mountains. 90 rooms. Major credit cards.

Sevilla

Alfonso XIII (5 star GL) $$$$$ *San Fernando, 2; Tel. (95) 422 28 50; fax 21 60 33.* Opened by King Alfonso XIII in 1929. This imposing hotel in the city center, set in its own lovely gardens, epitomizes Sevillian style and luxury. Classically decorated, spacious rooms, and a lobby bar that is a favorite meeting spot for Sevilla's high society. 149 rooms. Major credit cards.

Hotel Taberna del Alabardero (4 stars) $$$$ *Zaragoza, 20; Tel. (95) 456 06 37; fax 456 36 66.* A Sevillian mansion converted into a small luxury hotel with exclusive, personalized service. The rooms, named not numbered, are set around a patio and combine modern facilities with the classy elegance of an earlier age. 10 rooms. Major credit cards.

Hotel Los Seises (4 stars) $$$$ *Segovias, 6; Tel. (95) 422 94 95; fax 422 43 34.* An historic and beautiful 16th-century palace where historic surroundings combine with modern facilities to create an intriguing ambience. Central location in Barrio de Santa Cruz, with a rooftop pool overlooking the nearby cathedral and Giralda. 43 rooms. Major credit cards.

Doña María (4 stars) $$$$ *Don Remonelo 19; Tel. (95) 422 49 40; fax 421 95 46.* Charming hotel with an interesting mix of antiques and modern facilities. Excellent central location. A rooftop pool and bar are almost within touching distance of the Giralda and cathedral. 70 rooms. Major credit cards.

Patios de Sevilla $$$$ *Patio de la Cartuja, Lumbreras, 8-10; Tel. (95) 490 02 00; fax 490 20 56 and Patio de la Alameda,*

Alameda de Hercules, 56; Tel. (95) 490 49 99; fax 490 02 26.
Two typical buildings, in a bohemian district of Sevilla, converted into modern apartments with a bedroom, sitting room with
sofa bed, kitchen, and bath. Private parking. 56 apartments.
Major credit cards.

Hotel Monte Triana (3 star) $$$ *Clara de Jesús Montero,
24; Tel. (95) 434 31 11; fax 434 33 28.* Found in the quieter Tri-
ana area, across the river and just 10 minutes' walk from the city
center. Nice atmosphere and large modern rooms and public
areas. 117 rooms. Major credit cards.

Hotel Simón (2 stars) $$ *García de Vinuesa, 19; Tel. (95)
422 66 60; fax 456 22 41.* Fine, handsome hotel set in a reno-
vated 18th-century town house situated just across the street
from the cathedral. 31 rooms. Major credit cards.

Torremolinos

Tropicana Hotel & Beach Club (4 stars) $$$ *c/.
Tropico, 6, Box 29; Tel. (95) 238 66 00; fax 238 05 68.* Right
on the La Carihuela beach, this hotel has an interesting char-
acter with its own small garden and pool, beach club, and
prestigious Mango Restaurant. 85 rooms. Major credit cards.

Villanueva de la Concepción

La Posada del Torcal $$$ *Villanueva de la Concepción; Tel.
(95) 203 11 77; fax 203 10 06; e-mail* laposada@mercuryin.es.
A small, luxurious Andalucían country cortijo. On an isolated
hilltop, it has the rugged formations of El Torcal behind it and
the Mediterranean shimmering in the far distance below. Pool,
spa, sports facilities, and gourmet restaurant. 10 rooms. Major
credit cards.

Recommended Restaurants

The establishments recommended here are mostly traditional Andalucían restaurants serving local specialties. The resorts along the coast are packed with cheaper (and blander) alternatives, ranging from fast-food joints to Chinese, Indian, and Italian restaurants.

Seafood restaurants line the waterfront in every town, and are usually expensive — head inland a block or two and the prices drop considerably, though the quality remains the same. Reservations are recommended for the more expensive places.

Lunch is generally served between 1:30 and 4pm and dinner between 9 and 11:30pm, although restaurants in the larger resort towns tend to serve meals for longer hours. As a basic guide to prices, we have used the following symbols to give some idea of the cost of dinner for two, not including drinks.

$$$	over 10,000 ptas (€60.10)
$$	6,000-10,000 ptas (€36.06 - 60.10)
$	under 6,000 ptas (€36.06)

Benalmádena-Costa

Mar de Alborán $$ *Avenida de Alay, 5; Tel. (95) 244 64 27.* Near the marina in Benalmádena, this Basque-Andalucían restaurant specializes in good fresh seafood. Closed Sunday evening and all day Monday. Major credit cards.

Carmona

El Caballo Blanco$$$ *Plaza de Lasso, 1. Tel. (95) 419 10 00.* The à la carte restaurant of the Casa de Carmona hotel, set in the wonderfully renovated stables of this former palace. The tables, chairs, silverware, and crystal are special, and complement the classically prepared International and Andalucían dishes. A delightful dining experience indeed. Major credit cards.

Córdoba

El Churrasco $$$ *Romero, 16; Tel. (957) 29 08 17; fax 29 40 81.* Charmingly located in a 14th-century house in the Jewish quarter. Various dining areas are each uniquely decorated, with seasonal cuisine based on natural products and wines from its own Museo del Vino (Wine Museum). Closed August. Major credit cards.

Almudaina $$$ *c/. Camposanto de los Mártires, 1; Tel. (957) 47 43 42; fax 48 34 94.* A carefully restored 16th-century palace. Distinguished surroundings enhance the traditional Córdoban cuisine, which is prepared with fresh produce from the market. Closed Sunday night. Major credit cards.

El Puerto de Santa María

Las Bóvedas $$$ *c/. Larga, 27; Tel. (956) 54 04 40; fax 54 26 04.* Named for the vaults in the Hotel Monasterio San Miguel in which it is located, this is a unique restaurant. Typical Andalucían cuisine such as *pata negra* hams, and seafood delicacies like sea urchins au gratin.

El Faro del Puerto $$ *Ctra. de Rota, Km 0.5; Tel. (956) 85 80 03; fax 54 04 66; email* <elfaro_puerto@raini-computer .net>. Located in an old house surrounded by its own gardens, this restaurant is renowned for its creative cuisine that draws a balance between traditional and imaginative dishes and its extensive wine list. Closed Sunday night, except during August. Major credit cards.

Costa del Sol & Andalucía

Romerijo $, $, *or* **$$$** *Plaza de la Herrería, 1; Tel. (956) 54 12 54; fax 54 10 06.* In a city famous for its seafood, this is easily the most popular restaurant. Every conceivable variety of seafood and shellfish are served. Eat here or buy take-out from the *Cocedero.* Major credit cards.

Estepona

Lido Restaurant $$$ *La Boladilla Baja, Ctra. de Cádiz, Km 163.5; Tel. (95) 279 65 54.* Situated in the Las Dunas Hotel, this hotel has one of the finest reputations on the coast. Delightful decor, supreme service, beautifully presented Mediterranean cuisine created by a Michelin-starred chef, all accompanied by soothing piano tunes and magnificent sea views. A unique experience. Major credit cards.

Fuengirola

La Caracola $$ *Paseo Maritimo (Playa); Tel. (95) 258 46 87.* Found right on the beach, this restaurant has a relaxed ambience and serves specialties such as seafood casserole, small fried fish and fish baked in salt. Major credit cards.

El Madroñal

Mesón El Coto $$$ *Ctra. de Ronda (7 km from San Pedro); Tel. (95) 278 66 88; fax 278 88 90.* In the foothills of the Serrania de Ronda mountains and overlooking the coast, this is a lovely restaurant. Enjoy game such as rabbit, partridge, quail, duck, wild boar, and baby lamb or suckling pig, which you can cook for yourself on a stone. Major credit cards.

Granada

Chikito $$$ *Plaza del Campillo, 9; Tel. (958) 22 33 64; fax 22 37 55.* Typically Andalucían cuisine accompanied by a reasonably priced wine list in a city center location. Frequented by intellectuals and celebrities, whose photographs adorn the walls. Closed Wednesday. Major credit cards.

Las Tinajas $$$ *c/. Martínez Campos, 17; Tel. (958) 25 43 93; fax 25 53 35.* A popular meeting place, this restaurant specializes in local dishes with natural ingredients. Over 30,000 bottles of wine from Spain, France, and Germany. Closed July. Major credit cards.

Sevilla $$ *Oficios, 12; Tel.(958) 22 12 23; fax 22 96 29.* Granada's most famous restaurant, it was also once a favorite of García Lorca. The menu offers a good mixture of local Granadino and Andalucían specialties. Closed Sunday evening. Major credit cards.

Jerez de la Frontera

El Bosque $$$ *Avda. Alcade Álvaro Domecq, 26; Tel. (956) 31 20 20; fax 30 80 08.* Prestigious restaurant with elegant dining rooms adorned with classic taurine paintings. Traditional cuisine created with only the finest Andalucían products, and a wine cellar of around 25,000 bottles. Closed Sunday. Major credit cards.

Tendido 6 $$$ *c/. Circo, 10; Tel. (956) 34 48 35; fax 33 03 74.* Next to the Plaza de Toros, with a taurine name and décor. Typical Andalucían cuisine with a wide variety of meats, seafood, and shellfish dishes, and a mainly Spanish wine list. Major credit cards.

Málaga

El Chinitas $$ *Moreno Monroy 4-6; Tel. (95) 221 09 72; fax 222 00 31.* Attractive, traditionally-styled restaurant in the heart of the Old Town specializing in Andalucían and Málagueño dishes. Eat inside or at tables on the pedestrian-only street. Major credit cards.

Adolfo $$$ *Paseo Maritimo Pablo Ruiz Picasso, 12; Tel. (95) 260 19 14.* A restaurant with an agreeable ambience where you can enjoy high-quality creative cooking with a menu that changes according to the season. Closed Sunday. Major credit cards.

Bar Orellana $ *Moreno Monroy, 5; Tel. (95) 222 30 12.* No tables and chairs and just a small "L" shaped bar. However, the range and quality of the tapas are extraordinary, ensuring that it is hugely popular with Málaguenos, especially on weekends. Not to be missed. Cash only.

Antigua Casa de Guardia $ *Alameda Principal, 18; Tel. (95) 221 46 80.* Founded in 1840, and hardly changed since. Huge wooden barrels of local wines, especially the sweet Málaga dulce, sit behind long wooden bars. Be sure to taste the small dishes of prawns, clams, mussels, and other shellfish. Cash only.

Marbella

La Pesquera del Faro $$$ *Playa del Faro, Paseo Maritimo; Tel. (95) 286 85 20.* A charming restaurant in the La Pesquera chain. This one, in a central location on the beach, is a seafood lovers' delight. Wonderful ambience and sea views. Major credit cards.

Puerto de Banus

Taberna del Alabardero $$$ *Muelle Benabola, s/n; Tel. (95) 281 27 94; fax 281 86 30.* On the Main Quay overlooking the luxurious yachts, this is a prestigious and elegant restaurant. The menu features Mediterranean and Basque specialties, as well as international selections, and an extensive wine list. Open daily for lunch and dinner. Major credit cards.

San Fernando

Ventorrillo el Chato $$$ *Ctra. de Cádiz a San Fernando, Km 687; Tel. (956) 25 02 25; fax 25 32 22.* On the isthmus connecting Cádiz to San Fernando, this is a historic restaurant with an attractive Andalucían-style dining room. It has Andalucían-style cuisine, too, with tasty desserts and fine wines. Closed Sunday. Major credit cards.

Sevilla

Casa Robles $$ *c/. Alvarez Quintero, 58; Tel. (95) 456 32 72.* Very close to the cathedral in an 18th-century mansion, this restaurant is popular with locals and tourists alike. Expect traditional Andalucían stews and seafood dishes along with homemade desserts. Open daily. Major credit cards.

Egaña Oriza $$$ *c/. San Fernando, 41; Tel. (95) 442 72 11; fax 450 27 27.* In a beautiful building just across from the tobacco factory, this is a privileged location for a very prestigious restaurant. Renowned for dishes that combine Basque influences with Andalucían traditions. Spanish and international wine list. Closed Saturday lunchtime, Sunday, and during August. Major credit cards.

Mesón Don Raímundo $$ *c/. Argote de Molina, 26; Tel. (95) 422 33 55; fax 421 89 51.* Once a 14th-century convent, the décor here is emblematic of that era. Totally Andalucían menu, with large and small game specialties and delightful desserts. Major credit cards.

Horacio $ *c/. Antonio Díaz, 9; Tel. (95) 422 53 85.* Close to the Plaza de Toros. The ambience here is creatively modern, as is the Andalucían and international cuisine in this pleasing restaurant. Major credit cards.

Costa del Sol & Andalucía

Los Seises $$$ *c/. Segovias, 6; Tel. (95) 422 94 95.* In the hotel of the same name, this à la carte restaurant is actually set around Roman and Moorish walls and excavations. Specializing in the finest regional cuisine and desserts with Arabic influences. Major credit cards.

La Albahaca $$$ *Plaza Santa Cruz, 12; Tel. (95) 422 07 14; fax 456 12 04.* Three dining rooms in a typical Sevillian mansion, and al fresco dining in summer. A Basque-based menu offering exquisite dishes that change with the seasons. Closed Sunday. Major credit cards.

Corral del Agua $$$ *c/. Agua, 6; Tel. (95) 422 48 51; fax 456 12 04.* Found in a typically charming 17th-century house in the heart of the Barrio de Santa Cruz. Classic Andalucían cuisine enjoyed in tasteful dining rooms or outside in a beautiful patio around a fountain. Closed Sunday. Major credit cards.

El Rinconcillo $ *Gerona 40-42; Tel. (95) 422 31 83.* One of the oldest and most atmospheric tapas bars in the city, dating from the 17th century. A running account of your bill is chalked up on the wall. Major credit cards.

Torremolinos

Casa Guaquin $ *Carmen, 37, La Carihuela; Tel. (95) 238 45 30.* A block away from the promenade means lower prices in this fine seafood restaurant. Try the specialty, fried small fish and pepper salad. Closed Thursday. Major credit cards.

La Langosta $$ *Bulto, 53; Tel. (95) 238 43 81; fax 237 04 98.* On the Paseo Maritimo on the famous La Carihuela beach in the fishermen's quarter. Marine ambience, seafood specialties, wines from Spain, Germany, and France, and a menu in ten languages. Major credit cards.

INDEX